The Observers Series
DOGS

About the Book

Pedigree dogs are enormously popular and in recent years show entries have zoomed to figures never thought of even a decade ago. This attractive and enormously useful little book—written by an expert and one of the most experienced dog judges in the UK—gives basic details of 160 popular breeds (including some rare dogs more common in other lands). Each breed is illustrated by a colour photograph of a top show dog—representing a splendid collection of some of our greatest winning dogs. All the breeds represented can be seen at general championship shows round Britain.

The dogs are arranged in six groups according to their type: gundogs, hounds, terriers, toy dogs, utility and working dogs. Also in this volume are listed the breeds recognized by the English Kennel Club and the American Kennel Club, together with the winners of Best in Show at Crufts. A whelping chart is a very useful addition, there is a full index, and a glossary of technical terms.

About the Author

Catherine G. Sutton died in 1987. She had been involved with dogs for most of her life and was one of Britain's top dog show judges. In 1977 she judged Best in Show at Crufts. A dog breeder of great repute, Mrs Sutton owned over twenty champions in nine different breeds and for many years was the leading breeder of Beagles in the UK having had four different dogs win Best in Show at a General Championship Show. Mrs Sutton contributed regularly to the weekly magazine *Dog World* and wrote many books on dog matters. With her husband, she organized the Windsor and Richmond Championship Shows—two of the largest dog shows in the country with entries of over 9,000 dogs. She served on the Kennel Club Committees and gave the commentary in 1983 for the Group and Best in Show judging at Crufts.

The *Observer's* series was launched in 1937 with the publication of *The Observer's Book of Birds*. Today, fifty years later, paperback *Observers* continue to offer practical, useful information on a wide range of subjects, and with every book regularly revised by experts, the facts are right up-to-date. Students, amateur enthusiasts and professional organisations alike will find the latest *Observers* invaluable.

'Thick and glossy, briskly informative' – *The Guardian*

'If you are a serious spotter of any of the things the series deals with, the books must be indispensable' – *The Times Educational Supplement*

OBSERVERS

DOGS

Catherine G. Sutton

DESCRIBING 160 BREEDS AND VARIETIES

BLOOMSBURY BOOKS
LONDON

PENGUIN BOOKS

Published by the Penguin Group
Penguin Books Ltd, 27 Wrights Lane, London W8 5TZ, England
Penguin Books USA Inc., 375 Hudson Street, New York, New York 10014, USA
Penguin Books Australia Ltd, Ringwood, Victoria, Australia
Penguin Books Canada Ltd, 2801 John Street, Markham, Ontario, Canada L3R 1B4
Penguin Books (NZ) Ltd, 182–190 Wairau Road, Auckland 10, New Zealand

Penguin Books Ltd, Registered Offices: Harmondsworth, Middlesex, England

First published 1945
New edition published 1978
Reprinted 1980, 1983 (revised format), 1985
Reprinted with revisions 1987

This edition published by Bloomsbury Books, an imprint of
Godfrey Cave Associates', 42 Bloomsbury Street, London, WC1B 3QJ,
under licence from Penguin Books Limited, 1992

  3 5 7 9 10 8 6 4 2

Copyright © Frederick Warne & Co. 1945, 1978, 1983
Originally published as *The Observer's Book of Dogs* in small hardback format

Printed and bound in Great Britain by
BPCC Hazells Ltd
Member of BPCC Ltd

ISBN 1-8547-1093-1

Contents

Author's Note

In the pages that follow, we have tried to present to our readers good pictures of show specimens of the various breeds. As show dogs, in the main, are trained from a very early age to respond to lead and hand control from the handler, it is not easy to do without these controls in taking good pictures. This may help to explain why in some cases these appendages have been included.

Acknowledgements

The author and publishers wish to thank Diane Pearce for supplying all the photographs for this book, with the exception of the Airedale Terrier, Eskimo Dog, Leonburger and Bullmastiff, which were supplied by **Anne Roslin-Williams**. The front cover photographs were supplied by Diane Pearce.

Introduction

In rewriting this book, I have tried to bring it completely up to date and all breeds that are awarded English Kennel Club Challenge Certificates have been included. To become eligible for such certificates a breed must have registered no fewer than 150 dogs at the Kennel Club. Challenge Certificates are awards made at Kennel Club Championship Shows to the best dog and the best bitch in a particular breed. Three such awards under three Championship Show approved judges entitles the animal to become a Champion.

All breeds recognized by the American Kennel Club are also included, in addition to the better-known breeds in other countries. This brings the total number of breeds described to 160. It is hoped that the brief summaries and accompanying photographs will enable the reader to identify each breed that is dealt with.

Before selecting any particular breed of dog, it is most important to know at least what the dog should look like when he reaches maturity, as this knowledge can help one to assess adequately the housing and feeding requirements. Of course, when choosing a particular breed as one's companion dog, or even future show dog, it is assumed that the new owner is fully coversant with the likely cost of feeding, rearing and housing the animal. The most sensible place to buy any puppy or dog is from a reliable breeder. Here one can see the conditions in which the puppy has been reared and, naturally, see the puppy's dam and very often the sire. Any kennel owner will be only too happy to discuss all matters relating to the puppy's future and give advice to the new owner. It is as well to remember that the puppy or adult dog did not choose his or her new owner, but the new owner chose the dog. The dog is entirely the responsibility of his new master or mistress and most breeders will make this clear to the purchaser.

A great deal of time and patience is needed to rear

and train a young puppy. It is in these early months of his life that his character is formed, for good or ill. A well-reared and well-trained puppy is the envy of many and a very acceptable part, not only of his own household, but of the community generally.

When taking delivery of your puppy from the breeder, a diet sheet should be supplied and this must be followed carefully. When a puppy leaves a kennel, and his dam, it is a very big step in his life. No longer the familiar smells or the gentle hand that he has known so well. The new surroundings are completely strange, as are the voices of those around, and the routine of a household. The owner has to be very understanding at this stage to help acclimatize the puppy to his new home. Gentle, firm handling is required and it must be stressed that if the dog seems unwilling to settle at night, it is not a good thing, for the sake of peace, to take him off to bed with you. All puppies have enough common sense to realize when they are on to a good thing! It is necessary to have a hard heart on this particular matter, otherwise you will soon find yourself the slave of the puppy, and this does not make for a happy owner or dog.

It is not intended that this book should give details of how to train and rear your puppy. There are many breed books on the market that will apply to your chosen breed and these usually give full details for raising your pet.

If your puppy has come from pedigree parents the breeder should issue you with a pedigree and a form so that the puppy can be registered at the Kennel Club. If this has already been done by the breeder, you should be given a signed transfer form so that you may transfer the puppy to your name on the Kennel Club register.

It is essential that your puppy should be inoculated against hard pad, distemper, leprospirosis and virus hepatitis. This is usually done between 8 and 10 weeks of age. Until the puppy has been inoculated, he should not be exposed to any possibility of infection, and he should be kept away from all other dogs or places where other dogs have been exercised or housed. Two injections cover these various diseases and an appointment should be made with your local Veterinary Surgeon as soon as possible after acquiring the puppy. An annual booster is generally advisable after this.

Only the new owner can decide whether to select a dog or a bitch. If the latter, then it is important to realize that about twice a year the bitch will come into season. At these times it is absolutely essential that a careful watch is kept on her just in case she steals away to find a husband of her own choosing. Male dogs have a fantastic sense of seeking out a bitch in season, so do not think that because she is in her own garden minding her own business, some unwanted suitor will not find his way to her. She must be watched carefully during this period which lasts for about 21 days or even more. The most dangerous period during the season is from about the 8th day to the 14th day, depending on the breed. There is always a good boarding kennel that will care for your bitch during this difficult period if you find it impossible to cope yourself in your own home. It is much better to be sure than sorry.

If perchance your bitch is caught by some wandering male, it is essential to take her along to a Veterinary Surgeon straight away. An injection can then be given to stop her having crossbred puppies. Although this is the immediate solution to your problem, it is not altogether a very satisfactory answer as so often it upsets the bitch's breeding cycle. It does not, however, prevent her from having a perfectly normal pure-bred litter at some future date.

Whatever breed you may have, or are about to have, there is no doubt that properly reared and trained, the dog will give you many happy years of companionship, affection and loyalty. Prices for puppies are considerably higher than they were many years ago, but they are still relatively small when you consider the return.

1 GUNDOG GROUP
English Setter

This is a very attractive and elegant dog, with working
ability. The modern English Setter was greatly influ-
enced by the breeding carried out by Mr Edward
Laverack and Mr Purcell Llewellin in the 19th century.

A medium-sized dog with a long and reasonably
lean head with a well-defined stop. Body of moderate
length with short and level back. Tail should be set on
almost in line with back, of medium length and not
curly or ropy. The flag or feather should hang in long
pendant flakes. Coat should be slightly wavy, long and
silky. Breeches and forelegs should be well feathered.
Colour either black and white, lemon and white, liver
and white or tricolour. Height: dogs $25\frac{1}{2}$–27 in (64–
68·5 cm), bitches 24–$25\frac{1}{2}$ in (61–64 cm).

German Shorthaired Pointer

An all-purpose gundog descending from the Spanish Pointer, English Foxhound and local German tracking Hounds. A club to help foster the breed was established in the UK in 1951. This breed has now become popular in the show ring in Britain and is known for its excellence in the field.

A noble, medium-sized dog showing power and endurance plus speed. A short back standing over plenty of ground and with grace of outline. Head is clean-cut and neither too light nor too heavy. Ears are broad and set high. Neck is moderately long. Skin should not fit loosely or fold. Coat is short, flat and coarse to the touch. Colour solid liver, liver and white spotted, liver and white spotted and ticked, liver and white ticked, black and white. Height: dogs 23–25 in (58–63·5 cm), bitches 21–23 in (53–58 cm).

German Wirehaired Pointer

This breed is known in Germany as the Deutsch-Drahthaar and it is one of the most popular shooting dogs in its own country. They are slowly but steadily gaining popularity in the UK. They have come from the rough and smooth-coated pointing dogs in Germany and are now recognized as very versatile gundogs of courage and ability.

The coat is an important feature of the dog and the Drahthaar Club, in 1902, stated that the breeding of a correct wire coat is essential. This is easily understood when one realizes that this Pointer was designed as an all-weather all-purpose dog which had to negotiate underbrush that would severely punish any dog without such a coat. Colour is liver and white, usually spotted, ticked or roan but occasionally solid liver. Head, ears and nose brown. Height: dogs 24–26 in (61–66 cm), bitches less.

Gordon Setter

This black-and-tan Setter was first bred at Gordon Castle in Banffshire, Scotland, and is the biggest and heaviest of the Setters. It is thought that the Bloodhound and the Collie contributed to the Gordon's background as the 4th Duke of Richmond and Gordon desired a dual-purpose dog that was nearer to a Hound than to a Spaniel.

A stylish dog, built on galloping lines with a thoroughbred appearance. Head deep rather than broad. Tail carried horizontally or below line of back. Thick at the root, tapering to a fine point. Flag should be long and straight. Coat short and fine on head, front of legs and tips of ears. All other parts of body of moderate length. Colour a deep shining coal-black with no sign of rustiness, and tan markings of a rich chestnut red. Black pencilling allowed on toes and also black streak under jaw. Height: dogs 26 in (66 cm), bitches $24\frac{1}{2}$ in (61 cm).

Hungarian Vizsla

The National dog of Hungarian sportsmen and the only shooting dog of Hungary. Combines the duties of Pointer, Setter and Retriever on land and water. It is related to both the Pointer and the German Pointer. A very obedient but sensitive dog, easily trained and most affectionate.

Medium-sized, robust but not too heavily boned. The head should be gaunt and noble. Tail should be of moderate thickness, rather low set with one-third docked off. Gait is graceful and elegant with a lively trot. Coat should be short and straight, dense and coarse, and feel greasy to the touch. Colour russet gold. Small white marks on chest and feet are not desirable. Height: dogs 22½–25 in (56–63·5 cm), bitches 21–23½ in (53–59 cm).

Irish Setter

This dog came originally from Ireland and was probably created by crossing Irish Water Spaniels, Gordon Setters, English Setters, Spaniels and Pointers. In 1876 the Ulster Irish Setter Club ruled that in future the dog should be known as the Irish Setter. A very handsome dog with quite a bit of the Irish sense of humour in his make-up. More racy than the other Setters, his rich mahogany coat is most attractive. He has an excellent reputation as a working gundog.

Head should be long and lean. Eyes dark hazel or dark brown and not to be too large. Colour rich chestnut with no trace of black. Coat flat and silky with feathering on upper ear, back of legs, underparts, tail and between toes. No size is stipulated but overall balance is very important.

Irish Setter (Red & White)

The Red & White Setter originates from the Emerald Isle and is the forerunner of the Irish Setter, but the solid coloured reds became much more popular than the Red & White.

A dog of great power—athletic rather than racy. The skull should be domed (without showing the occipital protuberance as found in Irish Red Setters) and end in a fairly square muzzle. The dog must be clearly particolour, i.e. the base colour should be white with solid red patches. Mottling or flecking but not roaning is permitted around the face and feet and up the forelegs as far as the elbow and up the hind leg as far as the hock. Coat should be finely textured with good feathering. A slight wave is permissible but it should not be curly.

Italian Spinone

This old-established breed originated in France in the district of Bresse and from there spread to Piedmont in north Italy. The Barbet, the Porcelaine and the French Griffon are mentioned among its forebears. Later crossings with the Griffon Korthals and the Drahthaariger Deutscher Vorstehund were not very successful as far as appearance was concerned but it did improve the hunting capabilities and this suited Italian sportsmen who like to use the Spinone in marshy country and in woodland.

A big squarely built, rough coated dog with long ears and docked tail. Colour pure white or white with orange or brown markings. Body length equal to height at the withers. Loin well developed and slightly arched. Ribs long and well sprung. Quarters strong and well muscled.

Height: for dogs 23–27½ in (58–68 cm), bitches 22–24 in (56–61 cm). Weight: for dogs 70 to 80 lb (31–36 kg), bitches 60–70 lb (28–31 kg).

Large Munsterlander

The dog was created in Germany from the Hawking dog and the Land Spaniel. The Large Munsterlander is a multi-purpose gundog ideal for the rough shooter. He has an excellent nose, great stamina and works equally well on land or in water. A keen worker that is easily taught and is trustworthy. Alert and energetic with a strong muscular body. Good strong mover with drive.

Hair long and dense but not curly or coarse. Well feathered on tail, front and hind legs. The hair should lie short and smooth on the head. Head solid black, white blaze, snip or star allowed. Body white with black patches, flecked, ticked or a combination. Height: dogs 24 in (61 cm), bitches approx. 23 in (58·5 cm).

Pointer

The name of this dog is self-explanatory. The dog points out the game with his nose and was developed as a distinct breed earlier than the Setters. The first Pointers appeared in England about 1650 and were one of the two breeds at the first dog show held at Newcastle in 1859. Some say that the Pointer originated in Spain, but others feel that he was developed in this country by using Bloodhounds, Foxhounds and Greyhounds. Later the heavier Spanish Pointer was introduced.

The muzzle is somewhat concave, ending on a level with the nostrils and giving a slightly dishfaced expression. Tail long and tapering, and should lash from side to side in movement. Coat perfectly smooth with a good sheen. Colours are lemon/white, orange/white, liver/white and black/white. Self colours are also allowed. Height: dogs 25–27 in (63·5–68·5 cm), bitches 24–26 in (61–66 cm).

Portuguese Water Dog

Known in Portugal as the Câo de Agua Portugues. A
medium sized curly coated dog with long, wig-like top-
knot and curled tail. There is nothing definite about
his origin except he was formerly used as a hunting
dog and now along the whole coast of Portugal this
keen water dog helps the fishermen by retrieving lost
nets and tackle and guarding the boats. Colour is black
or black and white or brown or brown and white and
sometimes light grey, dark grey or solid white. Eyes of
medium size and black or brown in colour. Ears heart
shaped and set on above level of eyes and lying close to
cheeks. Short straight back with croup falling away a
little. This Water Dog makes a very obedient and good
guard. Ideal height: 20–23 in (51–58 cm), bitches
slightly less.

Retriever (Chesapeake Bay)

This is an American Breed of Retriever but bred from British stock. In 1807 an English brig foundered off the Maryland coast and the crew and two brown puppies were rescued by the American ship *Canton*. These puppies, Canton and Sailor, were used for breeding. Later their descendants were crossed with the Curly and Flat Coated Retrievers, plus the Otterhound, and in 1885 the Chesapeake Bay was created. These dogs were used for retrieving wild duck shot over the icy waters of Chesapeake Bay.

Head is strong with broad skull and medium stop. Eyes are medium large of yellowish colour and wide apart. A Chesapeake's coat should resist water and should be thick and short with a dense woolly undercoat. A curly coat is not permissible. Any colour ranging from a dark brown to a faded tan or dull straw colour. Must have a great love of water and a willingness to work. Height: dogs 22–25$\frac{1}{2}$ in (56–64 cm), bitches 20–23$\frac{1}{2}$ in (51–59 cm).

Retriever (Curly Coated)

This breed is one of the oldest of the Retriever Breeds. Unfortunately it is not so popular at the moment as the others. The origin is not known, but it is felt that this dog was a cross between the Water Dog and the early Labradors. He is a strong dog with great endurance and intelligence, loving the water.

His coat is distinctive and should be one mass of crisp small curls all over, black or liver in colour. The Curly Coated Retriever Club was formed in the UK in 1933 to look after the interests of the breed, particularly as working gundogs. The late Brigadier General Lance did a great deal to help the breed's survival. Height: 25–27 in (63·5–68·5 cm).

Retriever (Flat Coated)

This breed was originally known as the Wavy Coated Retriever and its sole purpose was to pick up the game. It was probably produced from the Newfoundland and Setters and/or Spaniels. A bright, active dog of medium size, and racy without being weedy.

The head is long and nicely moulded. The chest should be deep and fairly broad. Back should be short, square and well ribbed up. Hindquarters muscular. Tail short, straight and well set on, carried gaily but never much above the level of the back. Coat is dense, of fine quality and texture, and as flat as possible. Colour black or liver. Weight about 60–70 lb (27–31 kg).

Retriever (Golden)

The origin of this lovely breed has always created a certain amount of controversy. Research now seems to indicate quite definitely that the breed was started in the last century by the First Lord Tweedmouth, by mating a yellow wavy coated retriever to a Tweed Water Spaniel. The Golden Retriever Club was founded in 1918 and this is now one of the most popular breeds today.

A symmetrical, active, powerful dog with a charming kindly expression. He should never be clumsy or long in the leg. He has great working ability and makes a marvellous companion. His body is well-balanced, short coupled and deep through the heart. Coat should be flat or wavy with good feathering and dense, water-resistant undercoat. Colour any shade of gold or cream, but neither red nor mahogany. Height: dogs 22–24 in (56–61 cm), bitches 20–22 in (51–56 cm).

Retriever (Labrador)

This dog came from Newfoundland and is thought to have been brought over to Britain by fishermen about 1835. The dogs were used by the fishermen of Newfoundland to jump overboard and drag the ends of the nets through the water to the men on shore, who pulled in the nets full of fish. The dogs were landed at Poole in Dorset. The breed was first recognized by the English Kennel Club in 1903.

There are two distinctive features. Firstly, the tail which should be very thick towards the base and gradually taper towards the tip, clothed thickly all round with a short, thick, dense coat giving that peculiar rounded appearance which is described as the 'otter tail'. Secondly, the coat should be short and dense without wave and have a weather-resistant undercoat giving a fairly hard feeling to the hand. Colour is generally black or yellow, but other whole colours are permissible. Height: dogs 22–22½ in (56–57 cm), bitches 21½–22 in (54–56 cm).

Spaniel (American Cocker)

The Spaniel family is a large one and in the USA the Cocker Spaniel has been developed along different lines from English Cockers. In 1935, in America, a special club was formed for the American Cocker and the American Kennel Club recognized it as an independent breed in 1943.

The American Cocker is a small dog with a finely chiselled head. He has a very dense coat, much thicker than the English variety, and careful attention to stripping and trimming is needed. He was granted championship show status in this country in 1970.

His colouring is mainly the same as that of the English Cocker, but he is overall a smaller dog. Height: dogs 15 in (38 cm), bitches 14 in (35·5 cm). Weight varies from 22–28 lb (10–12·5 kg).

Spaniel (Brittany)

Brittany Spaniels were shown at the Paris dog show in 1900 and have been recognized by the American Kennel Club since 1931. Now one of America's most popular working gundogs. In its make-up are several different bloodlines including the old red-and-white Setter or Epagneul Breton, mingled with that of the Braque de Bourbonnais and the Italian Bracco.

A medium-sized squarely-built dog with moderately long ears and short, docked or natural bob tail. Muzzle about two-thirds the length of skull. A quick, very reliable worker which will retrieve in difficult conditions. Coat thick, flat or wavy but never curly. Colour white with dark orange or liver patches. Black or faded colour undesirable. Height: $17\frac{1}{2}$–$20\frac{1}{2}$ in (44–51 cm). Weight: 30–40 lb (13–18 kg).

Spaniel (Clumber)

This breed of Spaniel differs very much in type from the other members of this group. The Clumber is a massive Spaniel, not tall, but long in body and with tremendous bone. He moves with a rolling gait characteristic of the breed. Of French origin, the breed was developed at Clumber Park, the seat of the Duke of Newcastle, in Nottingham, from which he has adopted his name.

He works more slowly than the other Spaniels, but he has a certain dignity of his own and a very thoughtful expression. His colouring is attractive, plain white with lemon markings, orange permissible, slight head markings and freckled muzzle with white body preferred. Weight: dogs 55–70 lb (25–32 kg), bitches 45–60 lb (20–27 kg).

Spaniel (Cocker)

A very popular companion breed in Britain but only a few are trained to the gun. It is known for its very happy and gay disposition, and is often described as the merry Cocker. Spain is thought to be the country of origin and the dog goes back to the 14th century. The first field trial for Spaniels, to prove their worth as gundogs, was held in 1899 at Sutton Scarsdale and was promoted by William Arkwright. In 1902 the Cocker Spaniel Club was formed and a standard drawn up which has never been altered. In 1893 the English Kennel Club first recognized Cockers as a separate breed.

The Cocker should be well balanced and compact, have a good square muzzle and be of merry nature. Tail should be set on slightly lower than the line of the back. Coat flat and silky in texture, never wiry or wavy, with sufficient feather. Colours are various. In self colours—no white is allowed except on the chest. Height: dogs $15\frac{1}{2}$–16 in (39–41 cm), bitches 15–$15\frac{1}{4}$ in (38–38·5 cm).

Spaniel (English Springer)

The English Springer is the oldest of British sporting gundogs and the root from which all Land Spaniels, with the exception of Clumbers, have been evolved. In the Middle Ages the dogs were bred for finding and springing game for the net, falcon or Greyhound, hence their name. Nowadays this dog is used entirely to find, flush and retrieve game for the gun.

He is a symmetrical, compact, strong, merry, active dog built for endurance and activity. He is the highest on the leg and raciest in build of all British Land Spaniels.

Coat should be close, straight and weather-resistant, without any coarseness. Any recognized Land Spaniel colour is acceptable, but liver and white, black and white, or either of these colours with tan markings preferred. Height: 20 in (51 cm).

Spaniel (Field)

The Field Spaniel was developed in Britain for those sportsmen who wanted a heavier type Spaniel than the Cocker. This accentuation was nearly disastrous to the breed as the Field became very low to the ground, of great length and of a sluggish nature unsuited to his job. For the last 50 years, however, a much more workmanlike dog has been produced and today the Field Spaniel is enjoying much greater popularity in the show ring.

A well-balanced, noble, upstanding sporting dog, built for activity and endurance—a combination of beauty and utility, with a very docile nature. Head is most characteristic. The skull well developed with a distinct occiputal protuberance, not too wide across the muzzle which is long and lean, and lean beneath the eyes. Coat flat or slightly waved but never curled. A self-coloured dog, i.e. black, liver, golden liver, mahogany red, roan. Height: 18 in (46 cm). Weight: 35–50 lb (16–23 kg).

Spaniel (Irish Water)

This dog is of very ancient lineage, and was developed in Ireland. Often described as the clown of the Spaniel family and those who know him can understand this. A great character, very loyal to his owner but rather suspicious of strangers.

A medium-sized curly-coated dog with top-knot, long ringlet-covered ears and a characteristic rat tail. A grand water dog, he loves the water and is a strong swimmer. Although he may be a clown off duty, he is highly intelligent on duty and an excellent worker.

Coat is a rich dark liver having the purplish tint peculiar to the breed. Height: dogs 22–24 in (56–61 cm), bitches 21–23 in (53–58 cm).

Spaniel (Sussex)

This Spaniel is named after the county of Sussex where, at the end of the 18th century, he was first produced. Representatives of the breed competed in Britain as far back as the Crystal Palace Show of 1862. Although not as quick a worker as the Springer or Cocker, he has an extremely good nose and is inclined to give tongue on scent, which is not always popular!

Massive and well built, but active, energetic and strong, his characteristic movement is a definite roll which is unlike that of any other Spaniel. A reliable gundog, slow but steady. Coat abundant and flat with no tendency to curl and ample undercoat for weather resistance. Colour is rich golden liver and hair shading to gold at tips, the gold predominating. Dark liver or puce is objectionable. Height: 15–16 in (38–40 cm). Weight: dogs 45 lb (20 kg), bitches 40 lb (18 kg).

Spaniel (Welsh Springer)

This breed is also referred to in Wales as a 'Starter'. Very ancient and of pure origin, he was recognized by the English Kennel Club in 1902. A keen hard-working dog, on land and water, and a faithful and willing gundog. Overall he is slightly smaller and more refined than his English cousin, but he is easily distinguished by his colour which is rich red and white only.

Head is proportionate and of moderate length, slightly domed with clearly defined stop. Neck long and muscular. Body is not long, but strong and muscular, with deep brisket and well-sprung ribs. Tail is well set on and low, and never carried above the level of the back. Coat straight, or flat and thick, of a nice silky texture, never wiry or wavy. Height: dogs 19 in (48 cm), bitches 18 in (46 cm).

Weimeraner

The Weimeraner was originally a big game dog which seems to have come from the same stock that produced some of Germany's hunting breeds: Bloodhounds, St Huberts and Pointers. Nowadays the Weimeraner is used on various types of game and as a water retriever noted for his soft mouth. His distinctive colour of silver grizzle or mouse grey has scarcely changed.

His hunting ability is of the greatest importance and he should have a fearless temperament, be friendly, protective and obedient. A medium-sized grey dog with light eyes. Movement should be easy and co-ordinated. Coat short, smooth and sleek. In the long-haired variety the coat should be from 1–2 in (2·5–5 cm) on the body, somewhat longer on the neck. Colour preferably silver grey. Shades of mouse or roe grey are admissible. Height: dogs 24–27 in (61–69 cm), bitches 22–25 in (56–64 cm).

2 HOUND GROUP
Afghan Hound

The history of the Afghan is shrouded in mystery. The first specimen of the breed came to Britain from Seistan Province, Iran. It was named Zardin, and was brought here by Captain John Barff and exhibited at the Kennel Club Show in 1907.

Today it is common to have 400 Afghans exhibited at the large Championship shows. The Afghan is a real aristocrat and his whole appearance is one of dignity and aloofness. The king of dogs, with his eastern expression, he looks at and through one. His coat is dense and may be of any colour consisting of long silky hair of very fine texture. Along his saddle and on his foreface the hair is short. Height: dogs 27–29 in (68–73 cm), bitches 2–3 in (5–7 cm) less.

Basenji

The Basenji comes from Central Africa where he is used to hunt and destroy vermin. He does not bark, but utters a soft cry which is a mixture of a chortle and a yodel. The first specimens reached England in 1895 but did not survive for very long. They were re-established 20 years later, and in 1943 adopted the standard published by the English Basenji Club.

The Basenji has a wrinkled forehead, tightly curled tail, and legs that are carried straight forward with a swift, long, tireless swinging stride. A lightly-built Hound with fine bone. His wrinkled head with pricked ears should be proudly carried on a well-arched neck. Short, glossy coat. Rich chestnut with white markings. Can be tricolour or black with white markings. Height: dogs 17 in (43 cm), bitches 16 in (40 cm). Weight: dogs 24 lb (11 kg), bitches 22 lb (10 kg).

Basset Griffon Vendeen

This Basset is bred in the Vendée in south-west France
specially for coursing hares. A Briquet Griffon Vendeen is usually used for this sport but the landscape of
the Vendée is interspersed with roads and hedges
which, so often, are impassable in winter, and hunting
is on foot and not on horseback. The Basset Griffon
Vendeen is not quite so swift as the large Briquet and
so more suitable for this terrain which has to be hunted
on foot.

A short legged powerful, long bodied hound with
domed head and long folded ears. He has a strong
hunting instinct with good nose and a pleasing cry.
They are very affectionate and faithful and make very
good house dogs and companions. Height of the
Grande variety is from 15–17 in (38–43 cm) and for the
Petite variety from 13–15 in (33–38 cm). Colour: self
coloured. Bicoloured: white and black, white and grey,
white and red. Tricoloured.

Basset Hound

Large numbers of French Bassets Artesien-Normand were exported to England and it is generally accepted that these were the origin of the Basset Hound.

A compact short-legged Hound with a capacious but narrow and long skull and very long pendulous ears. The skin on the head should be so loose as to wrinkle noticeably when drawn forward or when the head is lowered. The breastbone should be slightly prominent, but the chest not narrow or too deep. Its mild and somewhat melancholy temperament is reflected in the expression. Any recognized Hound colour is acceptable. The coat should be smooth, short and close without being too fine. When the Hound moves, his stern is carried well up but is never curling or gay. Height: 13–15 in (33–38 cm).

Beagle

Little is known of his ancestry, but there is a reasonable certainty that the Beagle is one of the oldest of all pure-bred British Hounds. He has been a very popular Hound with many monarchs, and Queen Elizabeth had a pack of pocket Beagles reputed to measure less than 10 in.

Their work is to hunt the hare, but in the last 20 years they have become increasingly popular as companions. They have a very happy, gay temperament and are clean, tidy, small Hounds of great character. Coat is smooth and short and of any recognized Hound colour. Head is of fair length, powerful in the male and slightly finer in the female. Eyes are dark brown with a mild appealing expression. Neck must be sufficiently long to enable the Hound to come down easily to scent. Body should have ribs well sprung and extending well back. Loins should be powerful and supple. Tail of moderate length and carried gaily but not curled over back. Height: 13–16 in (33–40·5 cm).

Black and Tan Coonhound

This Hound is an American Breed and rarely seen outside the USA. It goes back to the Talbot Hound down through the Bloodhound and so to the Black and Tan Virginia Foxhound. A strong working Hound that works with his nose to the ground and is known for his deep voice when he has tracked his quarry. He is not expected to kill. Must be capable of withstanding the rigours of winter and the heat of summer.

The general impression is that of power and agility, but he has a very muscular neck. Ears should hang in graceful folds giving the dog a majestic appearance. Skin must be devoid of folds or excess dewlap. Coat should be short but dense to withstand rough going. Colour coal black with rich tan markings above eyes, on sides of muzzle, chest, legs and breechings with black pencil markings on toes. Height: dogs 25–27 in (63·5–68·5 cm), bitches 23–25 in (58·5–63·5 cm).

Bloodhound

The Bloodhound is a direct descendant of the old Celtic Hound and is one of the purest bred Hounds. He is a great tracker and, unlike police-trained dogs, he does not attack the man he is trailing. He possesses in a very marked degree every point and characteristic of those dogs that hunt together by scent.

A very sensitive Hound and rather reserved, his expression is noble and dignified, and his gait is elastic and free. Stern is carried high, scimitar fashion. Stands over a great deal of ground and is a very strong Hound. Skin is thick and loose, particularly about the head and neck where it hangs in deep folds; he has long hanging ears. Colour is black and tan, liver and tan and red. Height: 25–27 in (63·5–68·5 cm), bitches 23–25 in (58–63·5 cm).

Borzoi

The Borzoi has been used in Russia since the 17th century for hunting wolves and coursing hare and other game. The breed came to England about 1875.

He is a large, handsome and elegant dog possessing courage, muscular power and great speed. The back rises in a graceful arch with a well-balanced fallaway. Head long, narrow and clean. Tail long and rather low set with good feathering and should be carried low and not gaily. Coat is long and silky, never woolly, flat, wavy or curly. Short and smooth on head, ears and front legs. On the neck the frill is profuse and rather curly. Colours are not defined. Dogs from 29 in (73·5 cm) upwards. Bitches from 27 in (68·5 cm) upwards.

Dachshund (Long-haired)

Dachshunds were originally used to follow badger to earth and were called badger-dogs or dachshunds. It was not until the 19th century that they became known outside their native Germany. The Long-haired Dachshund was produced by crossing with the old Long-coated Spaniel. The Long-haired Dachshund is an old fixed variety of the Teckel. Long-bodied, short-legged and low to ground, he should never appear cramped in his capacity for movement. Head is long and should taper symmetrically. Forehead slightly arched and running into the bridge of the nose in an unbroken line without stop. Coat soft and straight or slightly waved and glossy. Coat should reach its greatest length on tail where it forms a flag. Colour black and tan, dark brown with lighter shadings, dark red, red, dappled, tiger-marked or brindle. Weight: dogs—middle weight up to 18 lb (8 kg), heavy weight over 18 lb (8 kg), bitches—middle weight up to 17 lb (7·5 kg), heavy weight over 17 lb (7·5 kg).

Dachshund
(Miniature Long-haired)

In conformation the Miniature Long-haired Dachshund should in all respects be similar to the Standard Long-haired. The body is compact, short-legged and long, well-muscled and strong. Eyes of medium size with a kind, intelligent expression. This small variety of Dachshund makes an excellent pet, particularly for those who wish to own a small, game, little Hound. Weight must never exceed 11 lb (5 kg).

Dachshund (Smooth-haired)

This very old German breed represents a combination of the dwarf Hound and the earth dog. The German Dachshund or Deutscher Teckelklub was founded in 1888, a German standard for the breed having been set up in 1879. (*See* Dachshund Long-haired.)

The Standard Dachshund is a short-legged, long-bodied dog of graceful build with a bold head carriage. The back is long, broad and muscular, and in the field of sport he is said to be unequalled, combining the scenting powers of a Foxhound with unflinching courage. Coat is short, dense and smooth, but strong. Colour can be any colour other than white (except a white spot on the breast). Nose and nails should be black. Large spots of colour on dapples are undesirable; the dog should be evenly dappled all over. Weight: dogs not over 25 lb (11 kg), bitches 23 lb (10 kg).

Dachshund (Miniature Smooth)

The standard of the Miniature Smooth Dachshund is identical with the standard of the Miniature Long-haired with the following exceptions.

Coat should be short, dense and smooth, adequately covering all the parts of the body and coarsest on the underside of the tail. The coat should never be woolly or curly.

Weight should not exceed 11 lb (5 kg), but the most desirable weight is 10 lb (4·5 kg). Any appearance of weediness or toyishness is to be avoided.

Dachshund (Wire-haired)

This variety of Dachshund came through cross breeding with the British Dandie Dinmont Terrier and the Miniature Schnauzer. It is said that the Wire-haired Dachshund is the sportsman's favourite. He is best suited for working purposes on account of his rough coat and undercoat. Like the smooth and long-haired varieties, his body is low to the ground and he can force his way through cover so dense that it would stop even the smallest gundog. Because of his nose, voice, good sight and determination, he makes an excellent tracking dog.

With the exception of the jaw, eyebrows and ears, the whole body is covered with an even, short, harsh coat plus an undercoat. He has a beard on the chin. Eyebrows are bushy and hair on ears is almost smooth. Weight: dogs 20–22 lb (9 kg–11 kg), bitches 18–20 lb (8–9 kg).

Dachshund
(Miniature Wire-haired)

The Miniature Wire-haired Dachshund is the most recent variety to be accepted by the English Kennel Club. His popularity is increasing and he is certainly a most appealing companion. For his size he is a great character, full of charm, affection and vitality.

Apart from the coat, the standard is identical with the standard of the Miniature Long-haired. The coat should be similar to that of his bigger brother the Standard Wire-haired. Weight must not exceed 11 lb (5 kg).

Deerhound

The Deerhound, as his name implies, is used to pursue and kill deer. One of the oldest breeds in Britain, Sir Walter Scott made frequent mention of the breed in his novels. In 1860 Birmingham classified the breed, and at Islington in 1869 four Deerhounds from the Royal Kennels were exhibited.

He is a very large, rough-coated dog with small drop ears and a low carried tail. A curl or ring tail is very undesirable. The hair on the body, neck and quarters should be harsh and wiry, and about 3–4 in (7·6–10 cm) long. The hair on the head, breast and belly is much softer. Dark blue-grey is the preferred colour, but darker and ligher shades of grey or brindle and sandy-red or red-fawn are also correct. Height: dogs not less than 30 in (76 cm), bitches 28 in (71 cm). Weight: dogs from 85 lb (38·5 kg), bitches 65 lb (29 kg).

Elkhound

The Elkhound is a fearless friendly dog from Norway who is devoted to his master and fond of hunting the elk. A member of the Spitz Group. It was not until 1877 that he was considered from a show point of view, and it was in that year that the Norwegian Hunters' Association held its first show.

The Elkhound is a compact and proportionately short-bodied dog with a thick and abundant coat and prick ears. The tail curls tightly over the back. His head is broad between the ears, and the muzzle is moderately long. The coat colour is grey of various shades. Weight: dogs 50 lb (23 kg), bitches 43 lb (20 kg). Height: dogs $20\frac{1}{2}$ in (51 cm), bitches $19\frac{1}{2}$ in (49 cm).

Finnish Spitz

For hundreds of years the Finnish Spitz was bred on farmsteads in Finland as a hunting and a watch dog. He is Finland's national breed and is mainly used for hunting forest birds.

The Finnish Spitz characteristics are eagerness to hunt, courage and fidelity. The breed was introduced into England in 1927, but is not yet acknowledged in the USA.

Colour on the back is reddish-brown or yellowish-red, preferably bright. The coat colour is lighter on other parts of the body. He has a bushy tail that curls over the back. Height: dogs $17\frac{1}{2}$ in (44 cm), bitches $15\frac{1}{2}$ in (39 cm).

Foxhound (English)

This breed has existed in England since the end of the
17th century. Today there are many fine packs of
Foxhounds in Britain, but they are never seen at the
Kennel Club shows. They have their own shows which
are governed by the Association of Masters of Foxhounds.

The Foxhound originates from the old and now
extinct Southern Hounds, the Talbots and the St
Huberts of the Ardennes. A medium-sized, strongly-
built Hound of strength and stamina. Should have a
good rib cage and a deep girth giving plenty of heart
room. His skull is broad and his neck should be long,
but not thick, as this would make him deficient in pace.
Colour is usually tricolour, black, tan and white, or
white with yellow or tan markings. The Masters of
Hounds say that no Hound can be a bad colour.
Height: dogs 23 in (58 cm), bitches just a little less.

Greyhound

The Greyhound is one of the most ancient breeds and has been used on practically all types of small game throughout his life. The hare is his natural quarry, and coursing the sport that he has been associated with for centuries. The Waterloo Cup was first run in 1836 and it is said that he can reach 50 mph (80 km/h) on a straight track.

The head is long with rose-shaped ears. The Greyhound is a strongly-built but graceful dog with a well-muscled long neck. The back is broad and exceptionally muscular with slightly arched loin. Coat is fine and close; the colour can be black, white, red, blue, fawn, fallow, brindle, or any of the colours broken with white. Height: dogs 28–30 in (71–76 cm), bitches 27–28 in (68–71 cm).

Hamilton Stovare

The Hamilton Hound is the most popular Foxhound
in Sweden. This dog was created by Count Hamilton
from the English Foxhound, the Holstein Hound, the
Hanoverian Haidbracke and the Courlander Hound.
In Sweden he is used for hunting various sorts of game.

The Hamilton Hound is a tri-coloured Hound,
black, brown and white, with no preponderance of any
one of these colours. He has a typical Hound head and
expression. Back is straight, strong and broad, and the
chest is deep. Quarters are very muscular and well
angulated. Coat is dense, strong and close-lying and
the undercoat is short, dense and soft. Height: dogs
19½–23 in (49–58 cm), bitches 18–22½ in (46–56 cm).

Harrier

The word 'harrier' is the Norman for hunting dog and was used in Britain until about 1750 as a collective name for all hunting dogs. About 1796 some very large packs of Harriers were kept in Devon, Somerset and Dorset. Harriers are never seen on the show bench in Britain today, but in America they appear regularly at shows.

A medium-sized hound with pendant ears and long tail. Very similar to the Foxhound. The coat is short, dense, hard and smooth, and of any recognized Hound colour. A strong, very agile Hound admirably suited for his job of hare hunting. Size varies from about 18–19 in (46–48 cm) right up to 21–22 in (53–56 cm).

Ibizan Hound

This Spanish Hound came originally from the island of Ibiza in the Balearic group, and is very similar in shape to the ancient Greyhound type. The breed has been kept very pure and is valued as a hunter. There are now about 200 registered with the English Kennel Club.

The Ibizan Hound is a tireless hunter who will retrieve to hand. He is a kind dog, but cautious with strangers. He has the ability to jump great heights without a take-off run. General appearance is that of a tall, narrow, finely-built deerlike Hound with large erect ears. Coat is either smooth or rough but always hard, close and dense. It is longer under the tail and at the back of the legs. Colour is white, chestnut, lion solid colour, or any combination of these. Height: dogs $23\frac{1}{2}$–28 in (59–71 cm), bitches $22\frac{1}{2}$–27 in (56–69 cm).

Irish Wolfhound

The Irish Wolfhound is the largest of the existing breeds and was once used by the Irish Kings to hunt wolves. After the extinction of wolves, the breed almost disappeared, but was rescued by Captain Graham who founded the Irish Wolfhound Club in 1885. In 1897 the English Kennel Club admitted the Irish Wolfhound to its register.

The Wolfhound is a very big, rough-coated Hound with proudly carried long, narrow head and small, Greyhound-like ears. The back is on the long side, with loins well arched. Coat is rough and hardy on body, legs and head being particularly wiry, and long over eyes and under jaw. The recognized colours are grey, brindle, red, black, pure white, fawn, or any colour that appears in Deerhounds. Minimum height: dogs 31 in (78·7 cm), bitches 28 in (71 cm). Minimum weight: dogs 120 lb (54 kg), bitches 90 lb (41 kg).

Otterhound

The modern Otterhound is, according to Stonehenge, a product of the 19th century coming from the Southern Hounds and the Welsh Harriers. Others have felt that the Water Spaniel, the Bulldog and the Bloodhound have a share in its creation. There are now no packs left in Britain today but this big hound is making very successful appearances in the show ring.

The Otterhound is a large, shaggy-coated Hound and is fast and untiring in the water. His webbed feet are of tremendous help to him in water. His coat is a double one with a water-resistant inner coat of short woolly hair, which is another essential feature of the breed. His outer coat is 3–6 in (7·6–15 cm) long on the back. Any colour or combination of colours is acceptable. The Otterhound is amiable and boisterous, but is an inquisitive Hound that likes to persevere in investigating scents. Height: dogs 24–27 in (61–69 cm), bitches are somewhat less.

Pharaoh Hound

The Pharaoh Hound is of great antiquity, bearing a striking resemblance to the Hounds with large erect ears depicted in the sculptures of the Egyptian temples dating from before 4000 BC.

The general appearance gives a strong impression of grace, power and speed. The skull is long and lean with the foreface slightly longer than the skull and only a slight stop. Eyes are deep amber in colour. The Pharaoh is an intelligent, friendly Hound—an alert keen hunter that hunts by scent and uses its large ears to a marked degree when working close. The coat is short and glossy with no feathering. Colour is tan, or rich tan with white markings. A white tip to the tail is desirable. Height: dogs 22–25 in (56–63 cm), bitches 21–24 in (53–61 cm).

Rhodesian Ridgeback

The Rhodesian Ridgeback is a native of South Africa. It is thought to have been created by crossing the Bloodhound with the native Hottentots. This dog is used to hunt big game, especially the lion, and he is capable of great endurance. The ridge along his back is his own special characteristic as the hair grows in the opposite direction to the rest of the coat. The ridge must start immediately behind the shoulders and continue up to the hip bones and must contain two identical crowns, but opposite each other.

Coat is short, dense, smooth and glossy in appearance, never woolly nor silky. Colour is wheaten to reddish-fawn. A little white on the chest is permissible. Height: dogs 25–27 in (63–68 cm), bitches 24–26 in (61–66 cm). Weight: dogs 80 lb (36 kg), bitches 70 lb (32 kg).

Saluki

The Saluki is perhaps the oldest known breed of domesticated dog as it can be traced as far back as 329 BC. The breed was officially recognized by the English Kennel Club in 1922 and the Saluki Club was formed the following year. This Hound is mainly used for gazelle hunting, for which its great endurance and agility is most useful.

The whole appearance of the breed gives an impression of grace and symmetry. The expression is dignified with gentle, faithful and far-seeing eyes. Ears are long and mobile with long silky hair. The neck is long, slender and supple. Tail is set on low and carried naturally in a curve. It is feathered on the underside with long silky hair. Coat is smooth and of a soft silky texture and can be white, cream, fawn, golden, red, grizzle and tan, tricolour, black and tan or variations of these colours. Height: 23–28 in (58–71 cm), bitches proportionately less.

Whippet

It is said that this breed was made in England sometime in the 19th century and it is almost certain that the Greyhound played an important part in its evolution. Whippet racing became very popular at the turn of the century when 300 dogs or more were entered in one handicap. The breed was not officially recognized by the English Kennel Club until 1890. The Whippet Club was formed in 1899 to encourage the showing of Whippets.

The general appearance should convey an impression of beautifully balanced muscular power and strength, combined with elegance and grace of outline. Head is long and lean and flat on top, tapering to the muzzle. Ears are small, rose-shaped and fine in texture. Coat is fine, short and close. Whippets make very attractive companionable dogs; they are friendly and affectionate in temperament and their coats are easy to keep clean. Any colour or mixture of colours is acceptable. Height: dogs 18½ in (46 cm), bitches 17½ in (43·5 cm).

3   TERRIER GROUP
Airedale Terrier

The Airedale is known as the King of Terriers. The breed originated about 100 years ago in Yorkshire and is thought to be a combination of the English Terrier and the Otterhound. During the First World War these dogs were used extensively as Army dogs and also for Police work.

A very affectionate dog and full of intelligence. There is nothing smarter than a well-trimmed Airedale. He has all the characteristics of the Terrier family and is the largest of this group of dogs. The skull should be long and flat, and not too broad between the ears, with only little difference in length between skull and foreface. Ears should be small and V-shaped. Colour is tan with black or dark grizzle body; the coat should be hard, dense and wiry, and not too long. Height: dogs 23–24 in (58–61 cm), bitches 22–23 in (56–58 cm).

Australian Terrier

British dog owners emigrating to Australia took with them their Scottish Terriers, Dandie Dinmont Terriers, Cairns, Fox Terriers and Skye Terriers and interbred them with great care to produce the Australian Terrier.

The breed was introduced into Britain in 1903, but was very variable in type; great improvements have been made to make it more uniform. The Terrier is a rather low-set dog, compact and very active. Its neck is long in proportion to its body. The coat is straight with hair from 2–2½ in (5–6.5 cm) long and of hard texture. Colour should be blue or silvery-grey on body; legs and face of tan colour—the richer the tan the better. Top-knot blue or silver. A second variety has clear sandy or red body with soft top-knot. Ears should be small, erect and pointed. Tail is docked. Height: 10 in (25 cm). Weight: 14 lb (6.34 kg).

Bedlington Terrier

The Bedlington is a very graceful muscular Terrier
with no sign of weakness or coarseness. He is capable
of galloping at great speed and should look as though
he can do this. A comparatively new breed, the name
was first applied about 1825 and originated from
Bedlington near Morpeth, in Northern England,
where he was used for ratting. The soft top-knot
suggests that he may have come from the same stock as
the Dandie Dinmont Terrier.

A medium-sized dog with low-set ears fringed at the
tip and a moderately long tail. His coat is very
distinctive, being thick and linty, and standing well
out from the skin. There should never be a tendency
for the coat to twist; this applies particularly to the
head and face. Colour should be blue, blue and tan,
liver or sandy. Height: 16 in (41 cm).

Border Terrier

This breed comes from the Border Counties of Scotland and England and is used for going to ground after fox. The Border Terrier is a very natural dog and is not docked. It may be trimmed, very slightly, simply to make the dog look tidy for the show ring. Essentially a working Terrier and a very game little dog.

Head is like that of an otter, moderately broad in skull with a strong short muzzle. The Border has a lovely keen expression; his ears should be small, V-shaped, of moderate thickness and falling forward close to the cheek. A deep and narrow body that is fairly long, with the ribs carried well back. Racy hindquarters with a strong loin. Colour red, wheaten, grizzle and tan, or blue and tan. Weight: dogs 13–15½ lb (6–7 kg), bitches 11½–14 lb (5–6 kg).

Bull Terrier

This Terrier is known as the 'gladiator of the canine race' and must be very strongly built and very muscular. Bred to fight, Bulldogs were crossed with lighter Terriers to produce the Bull Terrier. Later on, Dalmatian blood was introduced to give them a more streamlined appearance.

Head is very distinctive and should be long, strong and deep, right to the end of the muzzle. Viewed from the front it should be egg-shaped and completely filled. The eyes should appear narrow, obliquely placed and triangular. Colour, pure white and coloured, when the colour should predominate.

There are no weight or height limits, but there should always be the impression of maximum substance for the size of the dog.

Bull Terrier (Miniature)

These have never been very easy Terriers to breed and they are not seen in great numbers in Britain or abroad. They are a miniature of the Bull Terrier in every way with their courage and personality, and their own particular charm.

Height must not be more than 14 in (36 cm). Weight not more than 20 lb (9 kg).

Cairn Terrier

The Cairn Terrier has existed in the Highlands and Islands of Scotland since time immemorial. A very popular pet and show dog. The Cairn is a small, foxy, prick-eared, rough-coated Terrier and shaggy in appearance. He should impress with his fearless and gay disposition.

His head is small with a broad skull and a definite indentation between the eyes. He should have an abundance of hair on the forehead and a very strong jaw with a level bite. His original work was to rout out foxes and badgers from their dens. The dog should be double-coated, the outer coat being profuse and hard, but not coarse. The undercoat should resemble fur and be short, soft and close. Colour is red, sandy, grey brindled or nearly black. Must not be black and white. Weight 14 lb (6 kg).

Dandie Dinmont Terrier

The Dandie Dinmont is a very old Border breed that was named after one of Sir Walter Scott's characters—a sporting farmer called Dandie Dinmont who owned a pack of these Terriers. The first Dandie Dinmont Club was formed in 1876.

A long-bodied short-legged Terrier with pendulous ears and long tail. The back has a downward curve over the shoulders and an arch over the loin, with a very slight gradual drop from top of loin to root of tail. The coat is very important. The hair should be about 2 inches long. From the skull to the root of the tail there should be a mixture of hard and soft hair. The colour is pepper or mustard. Height from 8–11 in (20–28 cm). Weight 18–24 lb (8–11 kg).

Fox Terrier (Smooth)

This dog should present a generally gay, lively and active appearance, and have good bone and strength in a small compass. The Fox Terrier was created for use in hunting both fox and badger above and below ground. The Smooth variety reached a peak in its popularity towards the end of the 19th century. The English Fox Terrier Club was founded in 1875 and at that stage catered only for the smooth variety.

The head is relieved from being completely wedge-shaped by a little delicate chiselling. Ears small and V-shaped, and of moderate thickness, the flaps neatly folded over and dropping forward close to the cheeks. The coat is smooth, harsh and dense, and lies flat. White should predominate with coloured spots or patches. Weight: dogs 16–18 lb (7–8 kg), bitches 15–17 lb (6–7 kg).

Fox Terrier (Wire)

The Wire Fox Terrier followed the Smooth variety
and when the Wire Fox Terrier Association was
formed in 1913 it helped enormously to promote the
breed and to regularize the trimming of this Terrier
for the show bench.

Of similar shape and make to the Smooth Fox
Terrier, he is a very alert Terrier with a keen expression
and on the tip-toe of expectation at the slightest
provocation. His eyes, which should be dark in colour,
are full of fire and show his character. A very adaptable
companion showing affection and intelligence. Height
not to exceed 15½ in (39 cm) for males, the bitches being
slightly smaller.

Glen of Immaal Terrier

This is an Irish breed originating in County Wicklow in the glen from which it takes its name. This is a very tough terrier that has been bred to hunt the fox and badger. A very courageous terrier, daredevil but obedient and very attached to his owner.

Body is long with a broad chest and well sprung ribs. Legs short and strongly boned. The front legs may be slightly bowed. Tail is docked and carried high. Eyes brown with an intelligent expression. Coat harsh but soft rather than wiry and moderately long. Feet almost round and turned slightly outwards. Colour should be blue, blue and tan or wheaten. Size should not exceed 14 in (35·5 cm).

Irish Terrier

This Terrier is full of temperament and has a reckless air about him which is characteristic. A great sportsman, and fears no four-footed creature. He is known in his own homeland as the Red Devil. These Terriers have a great devotion to their masters.

Built on a racy outline, they must never be cloddy. Head is long with a flat skull. Eyes are not prominent but full of life and dark in colour. Ears small and V-shaped. Coat should be hard and wiry, and free of any softness. There should be no shagginess or curl. Whole-coloured, bright red, red wheaten, or yellow red. Weight: dogs 27 lb (12 kg), bitches 25 lb (11 kg). Height approximately 18 in (46 cm).

Jack Russell Terrier

This Terrier is not yet registered at the English Kennel Club as a separate breed. The Rev. John Russell, MFH (1795–1883), built up a strain of wire-haired Fox Terriers who used to run with his hounds, go to ground and bolt a fox from the crannies of Exmoor. Recently a Jack Russell Terrier Club has been formed and a breed standard drawn up.

The head should be strong boned with powerful jaws and level bite, and good strong cheek muscles. Eyes should be almond-shaped. Ears must be small V-shaped drop ears carried close to the head. The back to be straight with a high-set tail. Hind-quarters strong with good angulation. The coat is smooth or broken coated, but not woolly. The colour is basically white with black, tan or traditional hound markings. There are two sizes: one up to 11 in (28 cm) the other from 11 in to 15 in (28–38 cm).

Kerry Blue Terrier

Originally known as the Irish Blue Terrier when it was started round about 1912. It is thought that the Bedlington and Bull Terrier played a part in its development. Kerry Blues were classified at Crufts for the first time in 1922 and proved most popular. A compact medium-sized Terrier with a blue-coloured wavy coat that is soft and silky. This coat requires regular attention and care. The puppies are black in colour when they are born. Height: dogs 18–19 in (46–48 cm), bitches slightly less. Weight: dogs 33–37 lb (15–17 kg), bitches slightly less.

Lakeland Terrier

This Terrier comes from the English Lake District and was known as the Patterdale Terrier. Used as an earth Terrier, he worked with most of the hunts in his district. It was not until the formation of the Association in 1921, and the Lakeland Terrier Club in 1932, that he became known on the show benches.

A small, smart and workman-like rough-coated Terrier with small V-shaped drop ears. Fearless in temperament. Head is well balanced with skull flat and refined. Eyes should be dark or hazel. Coat should be dense, weather resistant and harsh, with undercoat. Colour is black and tan, blue and tan, red, wheaten, red grizzle, liver, blue or black. Weight: dogs 17 lb (8 kg), bitches 15 lb (7 kg). Height should not exceed $14\frac{1}{2}$ in (36 cm).

Manchester Terrier

This black and tan Terrier goes back to the old black and tan hunting Terrier. Most British Terrier breeds are rough-coated, but the Manchester is a smooth-coated dog. A compact dog with good bone. Head is long, flat in skull and narrow. Small dark and sparkling eyes oblong in shape but not prominent. Ears are small and V-shaped and carried well above the top line of the skull and hanging close to head. Coat is smooth, short and of a firm texture, and glossy. Colour is jet black with rich mahogany tan markings. Height: dogs 16 in (41 cm), bitches 15 in (38 cm).

Norfolk Terrier

The Norfolk Terrier has existed for many years and in 1932 the breed was admitted to the Kennel Club Register under the name of Norwich Terrier. There were two types—the erect ears and the dropped ears. In 1964 the Kennel Club agreed to separate them and the Norfolk Terrier became the breed with the drop ears.

One of the smallest of the Terriers, but a 'demon' for his size. A gay, smart little rough-coated dog always ready for some activity. He has great stamina and is a charming companion, affectionate and fearless. Head is foxy in appearance with the skull wide and slightly rounded and well-defined stop. Coat is hard and wiry and straight, lying close to the body; longer and rougher on the neck and shoulders. Colour all shades of red, red wheaten, black and tan or grizzle. Height: 10 in (25 cm).

Norwich Terrier

(*See* Norfolk Terrier for early history)

Like the Norfolk Terrier he is a happy gay Terrier, very active with a hardy constitution. A lovable companion with a fearless temperament.

The difference between the two breeds is that the Norwich Terrier carries his ears erect. They should be well set apart on the top of the skull, and of medium size with pointed tips. The ears should be held perfectly erect when the dog is aroused, but can be laid back when not at attention.

Colour, coat and size are similar in every way to the Norfolk Terrier.

Scottish Terrier

Up to the middle of the 19th century all dogs in Scotland that went to ground after the fox were known as Scottish Terriers. The breed was originally known as the Aberdeen Terrier. First registered at the Kennel Club in 1897 as a separate breed and known as the Scottish Terrier. A very attractive and affectionate companion, full of determination. Now one of the most popular of the terrier breeds.

A sturdy thickset dog of a suitable size to go to ground and a very keen working Terrier. Head long and narrow in proportion to the body. Eyes should be almond shaped and dark brown. Ears of fine texture and erect. The coat should feature an undercoat which is short, dense and soft. The outer coat is harsh, dense and wiry. Colour black, wheaten or brindle of any colour. Height: 10–11 in (25–28 cm). Weight: 19–23 lb (8·5–10 kg).

Sealyham Terrier

This breed was created in Sealyham, Haverfordwest, Wales, between 1850 and 1891, and developed from breeds known for their ability in quarrying fox and badger. They first appeared at a show in Haverfordwest in 1903, and in 1908 the Sealyham Terrier Club of Haverfordwest was formed. The breed was recognized by the English Kennel Club in 1911.

The Sealyham should be a free-moving active dog. Skull is slightly domed and wide between the ears. Jaws are very powerful. Eyes dark and of medium size. Mostly all white, or white with lemon, brown, or badger pied markings on head and ears. Height not to exceed 12 in (30 cm). Weight of dogs not to exceed 20 lb (9 kg), bitches 18 lb (8 kg).

Skye Terrier

The Skye Terrier goes back about four centuries and is practically the same today as he was in those days. The Island of Skye formed his native home, and there is no question that he belongs to the North Western Islands of Scotland where he was used extensively to bolt the fox and badger.

A one-man dog that is rather distrustful of strangers, but not vicious. The head is long with powerful jaws and a black nose. Ears prick or drop. Coat—undercoat short, close, soft and woolly. Overcoat long, hard, straight, flat and free from crisp and curl. Colour dark or light grey, fawn, cream, black with black points. Height 10 in (25 cm). Bitches slightly less. Weight 25 lb (11 kg).

Soft-coated Wheaten Terrier

This Irish breed has been known to exist in Ireland for at least 200 years and at one time these dogs were found on nearly every farm all over the country. In 1938 Dr J. D. Pierse had them registered by the Irish Kennel Club as a distinct pure-bred Terrier. In 1943 they were accepted by the English Kennel Club. They were shown at Crufts in 1949.

The Wheaten is very hardy and not exaggerated in any way. Medium-sized and full of confidence and humour. Head moderately long and profusely covered with a coat which should fall forward over the eyes. Eyes are a clear bright dark hazel. Movement is free, graceful and lively. Coat is abundant, soft and silky and never woolly or wiry. If curly, curls must be large and loose. Colour should be a good clear wheaten. Height: 18–19½ in (46–49 cm). Weight: 35–45 lb (16–20 kg). Bitches should be on the lower scale.

Staffordshire Bull Terrier

This Terrier comes from the old Bulldog-Terrier cross and was recognized by the English Kennel Club in 1935. Known in America since about 1870, and recognized by the American Kennel Club in 1935 under the name Staffordshire Terrier. This was altered in 1972 to American Staffordshire Terrier; these dogs are rather more heavily built than those in the UK.

The dog has indomitable courage, high intelligence and tenacity. The Staffordshire has great affection for his friends, particularly children, and is very much an all-purpose dog. Head is short, deep through, broad skull, very pronounced cheek muscles, distinct stop, short foreface and black nose. Smooth coat, short and close to the skin. Colour red, fawn, white, black or blue, or any of these colours with white. Any shade of brindle with or without white. Height: 14–16 in (35·5–40·5 cm). Weight: dogs 28–38 lb (12·5–17 kg), bitches 24–34 lb (11–15 kg).

Welsh Terrier

The Welsh Terrier is a very old breed and a descendant
of the old English Black and Tan Hunt Terrier which
greatly resembled a Miniature Airedale. Welsh Terriers are second to none as working terriers and they
are very robust and hardy. Easily trained to all sorts of
game and vermin.

The skull should be flat and rather wider between
the ears than the Wire Fox Terrier. Jaw is powerful
and punishing. Ears V-shaped, small, but not too thin
and set on fairly high. Coat should be wiry, hard, very
close and abundant. A single coat is wrong. Colour
should be black and tan for preference, or black grizzle
and tan, free from pencilling on toes. Black below
hocks is a fault. Height at shoulder should not exceed
15½ in (38 cm). Desired weight 20–21 lb (9–9·5 kg).

West Highland White Terrier

The West Highland White Terrier is said to come
from Argyll in Scotland. It was recognized by the
English Kennel Club in 1907, but as early as 1880 a
strain of cream-coloured and white dogs was bred from
the Cairn Terrier and by further selective breeding the
W.H.W.T. came to stay.

The Westie is a small, game, hardy-looking Terrier
full of his own self-esteem. This dog has a varminty
appearance combining strength and activity. The skull
should be slightly domed with a very slight tapering
from the skull to the eyes. Eyes should be widely set
apart, medium in size, as dark as possible in colour.
Coat is pure white and must be double coated. Open
coats are objectionable and the colour must be white.
Height about 11 in (28 cm).

4   TOY GROUP
Affenpinscher

This is a very old breed and was engraved on wood by Albrecht Dürer (1471–1528) and painted by Jan van Eyck (approx 1395–1441). Up till 1896 Miniature Pinschers and Affenpinschers were the same breed but had different coats. At the Berlin show of that year it was agreed that these two breeds should be separated and the wire-haired variety kept the name of Affenpinscher.

A very game, alert and sturdy little dog, he is the smallest of the Schnauzers and Pinschers, but well able to defend his master or mistress. Characterized by his 'monkey' expression which is accentuated by bushy eyebrows and moustache. The official American standard for the breed says that he should carry himself with comical seriousness, and this very aptly describes this grand little dog. In 1936 the breed was admitted to the American Kennel Club's Stud Book but so far only a few have been imported into Britain. Height: 9½–11 in (23½–28 cm). Weight: 7–8 lb (3–3·5 kg).

Australian Silky Terrier

This terrier is a native of Australia, although in fact it has been created by crossing the Australian Terrier with the Yorkshire Terrier. It was once called the Sydney Silky as it was developed in Sydney. In 1955 it became known as the Australian Silky Terrier.

The dog is compact, moderately low set, of medium length with a refined structure, but of sufficient substance to suggest the ability to hunt and kill domestic rodents. It should have terrier characteristics. The gait should be free and straight forward without any slackness. Coat must be fine and glossy and should measure about 5–6 in (13–15 cm) from behind ears to tail. Legs from knees and hocks to feet free from long hair. Colour blue and tan or grey-blue and tan. Height approximately 9 in (23 cm). Weight from 8–10 lb (3·5–4·5 kg).

Bichon Frise

This breed has recently been recognized by the English Kennel Club and also by the American Kennel Club (in 1972). The word 'bichon' is one used to describe the family of small, usually white, Continental dogs. This includes the Maltese, Tenerife Dog, Lowchen, Bolongese and Havanese.

The Bichon is a lively little dog with the coat falling in soft, corkscrew curls. The head carriage is proud and high. Eyes are dark, with dark eye rims and are full of expression. Ears hang close to the head and are well covered with tightly curled long hair. Tail is normally carried raised and curled gracefully over the back but never tightly curled. Coat is fine, silky with soft corkscrew curls. Colour is pure white and under the white coat dark pigment is preferred. Height should be less than 12 in (30 cm).

Cavalier King Charles Spaniel

Over the years the faces of these Spaniels grew shorter and shorter until they became more like those of dogs known today as the King Charles Spaniel. In 1926 an American, Mr Roswell Eldridge, was so disappointed in this new type that he offered a prize at Crufts of £25 for the best specimen exhibited in a class for Blenheim Spaniels of the old type. This prize was offered yearly for five years and encouraged breeders to breed back the long noses. In 1928 the Cavalier King Charles Spaniel Club was registered. Separate registration was granted by the English Kennel Club in 1945.

The Cavalier's head is almost flat between the ears and without dome. Ears are set fairly high and the muzzle is long with a very shallow stop. An active, graceful and well-balanced dog, very sporting in character. Coat is long, silky and free from curl, with feathering on legs, ears and tail. Colour black and tan, ruby, blenheim and tricolour. Weight: 12–18 lb (5–8 kg).

Chihuahua (Long Coat)

This is basically the same make and shape as the smooth-haired variety with the exception of the coat. Both varieties can appear in the same litter. The coat is long and of soft texture, either flat or slightly wavy. No tight curly coat. There should be feathering on the feet and legs, pants on the hind legs; a large ruff on the neck is desired and preferred. The tail should be long and full as a plume.

Since 1964 the two varieties have been divided into separate breeds in Britain. Like the smooth-coated variety, the ears on this diminutive little breed are large and set on at an angle of about 45 degrees giving breadth between the ears.

Chihuahua (Smooth Coat)

The Chihuahua is thought to be the smallest dog in the world. Of Mexican origin, it descended from the sacred dog of the Aztecs and was developed in the USA. The first Chihuahua reached America about 1900 and a specialist Club was formed in 1943. Breeding started in Britain about 1949 with stock imported from America. Now the Chihuahua is one of the most popular Toy breeds.

A swift-moving little dog with a saucy expression. Small, dainty and compact, with forceful action. The head is a characteristic of this breed as it should have an apple-domed skull with a molero—an area in which the skull bones have failed to join. Coat is smooth, of soft texture, close and glossy. Any colour or mixture of colours. Weight: up to 6 lb (2·5 kg) permissible, but 2–4 lb (1 kg–2 kg) preferable.

Chinese Crested Dog

This little dog is one of the varieties of the Hairless dogs which are to be found in many parts of the world. They are usually pricked-eared and either completely devoid of hair, or nearly hairless. The skin is hot to the touch and although it has never been ascertained why there is lack of coat, it has been found that hairlessness is sex-linked to lack of teeth, which is found in many of the specimens. Their body temperature is about four degrees higher than that of humans.

The Chinese Crested Dog has been accepted on the register of the English Kennel Club. A small, active and graceful dog, medium to fine boned, smooth hairless body with hair on feet, head and tail only. It can be any colour—plain or spotted. Weight from 7–12 lb (3–5·5 kg).

English Toy Terrier
(Black and Tan)

This is a miniature form of the Manchester Terrier and is in fact a toy dog with terrier characteristics. This breed started in England as Toy Manchester Terriers, then became Toy Black and Tans and so to Miniature Black and Tans. In 1962 they were recognized by the English Kennel Club as English Toy Terriers (Black and Tan). It is essential that these little dogs should be game and fearless in temperament.

The head should be long and narrow with a flat skull. Ears should be 'candle-flame' shape, slightly pointed at the tips and placed high upon the back of the skull. The ear carriage must be erect. Coat texture should be thick, close, smooth and of a glossy appearance. Colour—black and tan, and the colours should not run or blend into each other but should meet abruptly. Tan should be on fore-legs, muzzle, throat, inside of hind legs and under tail. Height: 10–12 in (25–30 cm). Ideal weight: 6–8 lb (3–4 kg).

Griffon Bruxellois

This breed came to Britain from Belgium towards the end of the last century where they were used as ratters. There are two varieties. The rough-coated, which is known as the Bruxellois and the smooth-coated, the Petit Brabançon. Both have a pert monkey-like expression and are full of character, but rather diffident with strangers.

They are highly intelligent, well-balanced square little dogs, very lively and alert. Head should be large and round, but in no way domed, and there should be a deep stop between nose and skull. Chin is prominent and mouth slightly undershot but teeth should not be visible. Coat in the rough variety is harsh, wiry and free from curl. Smooth variety short and tight. Colour clear red, black or black and rich tan. Weight: 5–11 lb (2–5 kg).

Italian Greyhound

This is really a miniature Greyhound, more slender in all proportions and of real elegance and grace in shape, symmetry and action. Brought to Britain during the early years of the 17th century. The high stepping action is a characteristic of the breed.

The skull is long, flat and narrow. Muzzle very fine. Ears rose-shaped and placed well back. Chest is deep and narrow, back curved and drooping at the hindquarters. The bone should be slender and delicate. Coat is fine and supple with thick and glossy hair. All shades of fawn, white cream, blue, black and fawn, and white pied are permissible. Weight: from 6–8 lb (2·5–3·5 kg) and not exceeding 10 lb (4·5 kg). Black or blue with tan markings and brindle are faults.

Japanese Chin

This Toy breed first came to England about 1860. It is a very old breed, borne out by the fact that similar dogs have been noted on the old Chinese temples.

A very decorative breed, dainty in appearance, with smart, compact carriage and profuse coat. The skull is broad and rounded in front, but in no way domed. The eyes are very important and it is desirable that the white shows in the inner corners giving the Japanese Chin the characteristic look of astonishment, which should on no account be lost. Coat is profuse, long and soft and straight, of silky texture. Colour can be black and white or red and white. The daintier the better but on no account should type, quality and soundness be sacrificed.

King Charles Spaniel

The history of the King Charles Spaniel is lost in obscurity. The Spaniel enjoyed tremendous popularity during the Edwardian reign, but in recent years it has unfortunately declined in numbers. The King Charles is divided into four varieties according to colour: the Blenheim, the Ruby, the Tri-colour and the Black and Tan.

It is a compact and cobby dog, built on refined lines, with wide deep chest and short straight legs, back short and level. Tail well flagged but not carried over the back. Head is quite different from the Cavalier as his skull is massive in comparison to size and is well domed and full over the eyes. The nose is very short and up-turned to meet the skull with a deep stop. Most desirable weight 8–14 lb (3·5–6 kg). This is less than the Cavalier.

Löwchen

This dog is often referred to as the Little Lion Dog because the body is clipped in the traditional lion clip and the tail, also clipped, is topped with a plume, thus giving the dog the appearance of a little lion.

Sufficient registrations were obtained in Britain in 1975 for the breed to qualify for Kennel Club Challenge Certificates in 1976.

The Löwchen is a member of the Bichon family and any colour is permissible be it self colour or part-colour. The most popular colours are white, black and lemon. A most intelligent little dog that makes a very good companion. Weight: 8–9 lb (3·5–4 kg).

Maltese

As indicated by the name, this dog has been very prominent in Malta for many centuries and is the oldest of the European Toy breeds.

A charming sweet-tempered toy breed with great intelligence. Head is well balanced and nose should be pure black. Eyes should be dark brown with black eye rims. Body short and cobby and back straight. Tail should arch over the back and be feathered. Coat should be of good length, but not impeding action, of silky texture and not in any way woolly. It should be straight. The colour is pure white but slight lemon markings should not penalize. Size not over 10 in (25 cm).

Miniature Pinscher

Dogs of this type can be traced for about 300 years and although they bear a resemblance to the Dobermann Pinscher, they are a much older breed than the Dobermann. A well-balanced sturdy compact short-coupled smooth-coated toy dog, with a precise hackney gait that is most characteristic. A fearless little toy dog with complete self-possession and spirit.

Head is more elongated than short and round with strong muzzle. Tail is docked but is a continuation of the top-line and carried a little high. Coat smooth and hard and short. Colour black, blue, chocolate with sharply defined tan markings. Height: 10–12 in (25–30 cm).

Papillon

This dog was known in the 16th century as the Dwarf
Spaniel and seemed to originate in Spain, although it
was also known in France and Italy. Papillon is the
French for 'butterfly', hence the name for this little dog
whose ears are set obliquely on the head and are so
fringed that they resemble the wings of a butterfly.
Another variety of the breed has drop ears and is
known as Phalenes (moth). Ears must be completely
erect or dropped.

A very dainty, gay, balanced little dog with an
attractive head and intelligent, lively expression. Coat
should be abundant, long, silky and fine with no
undercoat. They make charming companions. The
dog should appear slightly longer than high when in
full coat. Colour should be white with patches of any
colour except liver. Ideal height 8–11 in (20–28 cm).

Pekingese

This breed has a very distinctive personality, probably gained centuries ago when it was a great favourite with the Chinese Court. These dogs were first introduced to Britain in 1860 after the sacking of the Summer Palace in Peking.

A small, well-balanced thickset dog of great dignity and quality. Head is massive with broad skull, but wide and flat between the ears. Nose is very short and broad with large nostrils. Eyes large, clear, dark and lustrous. Body is short with good spring of rib. Feet are large and flat; front feet slightly turned out. The gait is characteristic of the breed and should indicate a slow rolling gait in front with a close gait behind. Tail set high and carried tightly, slightly curved over back to either side. Long feathering. Coat long and straight with profuse mane extending beyond shoulders. All colours are acceptable. Weight: dogs not over 11 lb (5 kg), bitches 12 lb (5·5 kg).

Pomeranian

This Toy dog is a member of the Spitz family which came originally from the Arctic Circle. The breed arrived in England about 100 years ago and the British breeders have brought it to a very high standard of perfection. A compact, short-coupled little dog, full of spirit and character. Head is foxy in outline with small erect ears. Body is short with well-rounded ribs. Tail is one of the characteristics of the breed and should be turned over the back and carried flat and straight; profusely covered with long, harsh, spreading hair.

There should be two coats: one a short fluffy undercoat, and the other a long, perfectly straight coat covering the whole of the body and being very abundant round the neck—forming a frill. Colour can be any whole colour free from black or white shadings. Weight: dogs 4–4½ lb (1·5–2 kg), bitches 4½–5½ lb (2–2·5 kg).

Pug

Like most of the other short-faced dogs with curled tails the Pug came from China, but became very popular in Holland. It was from there that dogs were imported into Britain.

A great character, the Pug is often described as *Multum in parvo* as he is a decidedly square and cobby dog, with well-knit proportions and good muscular development. Head is large, massive and round, but never apple-headed. Muzzle is short, blunt, square but not upfaced. The wrinkles are deep and large. Eyes are bold and prominent with a soft appealing expression. Tail must be tightly curled over the hip; a double curl is much desired. Coat fine, smooth, soft, short and glossy. Colours can be silver, apricot-fawn or black. The ears, mask and trace (a black line extending from the top of the head to tail) should be black and clearly defined. Weight: 14–18 lb (6–8 kg).

Yorkshire Terrier

According to English Kennel Club registrations this is the most popular toy dog in Britain today and is considered to be an entirely English product. These dogs are born black and the desired steel-blue colour appears as they mature.

The coat is of tremendous importance and should hang quite straight and evenly down each side, and be of a dark steel-blue. A parting extends from the nose to the end of the tail. In full coat this dog is most glamorous and has very many admirers. His upright carriage is of great importance and he has a well-proportioned body. Head is small and flat with a black nose; the fall on the head is a rich golden tan, deeper in colour at the sides of the head and on the muzzle, where it should be very long. Tan on head should never extend on to the neck. Hair on chest is a rich bright tan. All tan hair should be darker at the roots than in the middle. Weight up to 7 lb (3 kg).

5   UTILITY GROUP
Boston Terrier

This is an American native breed and the result of a cross between the British Bulldog and a white English Terrier. In 1891 the Boston Terrier Club of America was formed and the name of the breed established.

The Boston is a great little character full of life, highly intelligent, smooth-coated, short-headed, compactly built with short tail. A balanced dog of medium size, brindle in colour, and evenly marked with white. Skull is square and flat on top being free from wrinkle and with flat cheeks. Stop is well defined. Muzzle short, square, wide and deep, and in proportion to skull. Eyes wide apart, large and round, and dark in colour. Ears are carried erect. Coat short, smooth, bright and fine in texture. Colour brindle with white markings. Brindle must show throughout the body. Weight: not more than 25 lb (11·5 kg).

Bulldog

This dog is a descendant of the old bull-baiting dogs once used in England for this sport. Bull-baiting was abolished in 1838 and since then the appearance of the Bulldog has improved. The Bulldog Club was founded in 1864 and the breed was recognized by the English Kennel Club in 1875.

The Bulldog is a smooth-coated thickset dog, rather low in stature but broad, powerful and compact. Head is massive and large in proportion to the dog's size, with an undershot jaw that projects in front of the upper jaw. British breeders have transformed the fighting and bull-baiting dog into a charming good-natured animal that is sensible and quiet. When aroused, he can defend himself and his owner with great tenacity. Coat fine in texture, short, close and smooth. Any colour is permitted except dudley, black and black and tan. Weight: dogs 55 lb (25 kg), bitches 50 lb (23 kg).

Chow Chow

This is a Chinese breed more than 2000 years old. The Chow is rather an aloof dog and belongs to the Spitz family; it has a peculiar bluish-black tongue. A balanced dog, leonine in appearance with a very proud, dignified bearing. Short coupled in conformation, he has a well-knit frame and carries his tail well over the back. Hocks are straight, with no angulation, giving the Chow his rather stilted gait which is a characteristic of the breed.

The outer coat is coarse, with a soft woolly undercoat. On the neck, shoulders and nape the coat should be as long as possible to form a mane. The smooth-coated Chow is similar in all respects except that its coat is short, being only about $1\frac{1}{2}$ in (3 cm) in length. Colour is whole coloured: black, red, blue, fawn, cream or white. Height: 18 in (45·5 cm).

Dalmatian

It is thought that the breed came to Britain from Yugoslavia, but it is the British breeders who undoubtedly have brought them up to today's high standard. They were used as coach dogs, but have also taken part in many other activities. The Dalmatian is a strong, muscular, active dog of good temperament, free from all coarseness and capable of great endurance, with a fair amount of speed.

Coat should be short, hard and dense, sleek and glossy in appearance. The ground colour is pure white. Black-spotted dogs should have dense black spots and liver-spotted dogs liver-brown spots. These should not run together but be round and well defined. Spots on the extremities should be smaller than those on the body. It is a bad fault to have patches of black and liver spots on the same dog. Puppies are born white. Height: dogs 23–24 in (58–61 cm), bitches 22–23 in (56–58 cm).

French Bulldog

The French consider this to be one of their native dogs.
Some feel that it is descended from the Bulldog, but
any British efforts to breed small sound Bulldogs were
not successful. In 1894 Mr Krehl imported several
small active Bulldogs, with upstanding ears, from
France. In 1902 the French Bulldog Club of England
was formed to look after the interests of this breed.

The French Bulldog has two distinctive features:
the bat ears and its skull which, if correctly formed,
should be nearly flat between the ears with a domed
forehead. The tail is short and thick at the root. Coat is
of fine texture, smooth, glossy and short. The permitted
colours are brindle, pied and fawn. Weight: dogs 28 lb
(12·5 kg), bitches 24 lb (11 kg).

Japanese Akita

The Akita is the national breed of Japan and was originally used for hunting game. A most impressive, powerful animal of the Spitz Group with a short coat and small prick ears that are set high and carried erect well forward over the eyes. A short back with a deep chest that is well rounded. Tail is set on high and carried over the rump, either curved or curled, with the tip hanging downward over the thigh and profusely covered with hair. Coat colour can be deer red, white, wheaten, black, greyish-brown, ash-grey, silver-grey, steel-blue, black and tan or brindle. A very reliable guard and protector of his own property.

Height: dogs 25–27½ in (63–69 cm), bitches 23–25 in (58–63 cm).

Japanese Spitz

The Japanese Spitz, as its name implies, comes from Japan and is a most attractive pure white, lively and bold small dog.

This dog should have a sharply pointed muzzle and triangular shaped ears standing erect. Bushy tail carried over the back. The overall quality of the body should be firm and strong and full of flexibility.

Head of medium size without any coarseness and moderately broad and slightly rounded. Skull should be broadest at the occiput with a well defined stop and rounded cheeks. Forehead not protruding. Lips should be firm and tightly closed with black colour desirable. The nose round and small and black in pigmentation. Neck should be strong and of moderate length. Chest is broad and deep with ribs powerfully sprung and belly moderately firm with good tuck-up. Hindquarters muscular and moderately angulated.

Outer coat should be straight and stand-off with profuse undercoat. Height: 12–16 in (30–40 cm) for males, 10–14 in (25–35 cm) for females.

Keeshond

This is the Dutch National Breed and in many ways similar to the Wolf Spitz. The Keeshond was originally the barge and watchdog. During the unrest preceding the French Revolution, the Patriots were led by a man named Kees de Gyselaer. This man was a great dog lover and owned a little dog called Kees. He became the symbol of the Patriots and gave the breed its name. The breed was brought to England by Mrs Wingfield Digby.

A short, compact body with an alert carriage and foxlike head. A large ruff on the neck and a well-feathered tail that is carried over the back. Movement should be brisk and sharp. Coat should be dense and harsh with profuse trousers. Colour wolf, ash-grey. Height: dogs 18 in (45·5 cm), bitches 17 in (43 cm).

Leonberger

This breed has been created through the crossing of a St Bernard with a Landseer Newfoundland, and interbreeding the progeny with a Pyrenean Mountain Dog. The result of this is a very handsome golden-coloured long-coated dog, with drop ears and a bushy tail. One was brought to England after the war and shown at Crufts and several now appear in the show ring in Britain. They are mainly seen in Germany but can also be found elsewhere on the Continent. Various shades of yellow are preferred with a black mask. Size 30 in for dogs (76 cm), bitches from 27 in (68 cm).

Lhasa Apso

The Apso comes from Tibet and is known in its own land as Abso Seng Kye, 'Bark Lion Sentinel Dog'. These dogs were first introduced into England by the Hon. Mrs Bailey in 1928. They now give big entries at major shows, and their gay, charming manners have found many devotees.

The Lhasa is a well-balanced solid dog with a free and jaunty movement. Head should have heavy furnishings, with a good fall over the eyes, plus whiskers and beard. The body should be longer than it is high, with a level topline. Top coat is heavy, straight and hard, not woolly or silky, with a dense undercoat. The colour is golden, sandy, honey, dark grizzle, slate, smoke, parti-colour, black, white or brown. Ideal size 10 in (25 cm) for dogs, bitches slightly less.

Poodle (Standard)

The French, Germans and Russians all stake their claims in the history of this popular breed. One of the first references to a Poodle in England appears in 1635, when Prince Rupert came to aid Charles I and brought his Poodle with him. The first Poodles were registered at the English Kennel Club in 1875 and continued to gain great popularity.

The Standard is a very active, intelligent and elegant-looking dog that carries himself proudly. The coat is very profuse and can be clipped to suit different tastes. All solid colours are permitted. Height: 15 in (38 cm) and over.

Poodle (Miniature)

The Miniature Poodle should in every way be a replica, in miniature, of the Standard Poodle. This variety was first registered at the English Kennel Club in 1911, and in 1954 there were more registrations at the Kennel Club than for any other breed. The Miniature Poodle's rise to popularity was quite fantastic and this breed stayed at the top of the registration tree for several years. In America the same popularity existed; they had definitely become established as favourites with dog lovers throughout the world.

The Miniature Poodle must not exceed 15 in (38 cm) in height and should not be under 11 in (28 cm).

Poodle (Toy)

This variety of Poodle has been bred down from the Standard Poodle through the Miniature Poodle. By the middle of the 1950s this breed had so progressed in numbers that the English Kennel Club granted it a separate register. This was also the case in America, but there it was ruled that the Toy Poodle should be under 10 in (25·5 cm) in height. In Britain the English Kennel Club set the height at 11 in (28 cm) at the shoulder.

The standard is exactly similar in all respects for the Toy Poodle as it is for its bigger relations, apart from the question of size. It must come below 11 in (28 cm) at the shoulder.

Like the Miniature, the Toy has revelled in its great popularity both in this country and across the ocean.

Schipperke

The Schipperke originated in the Flemish provinces of Belgium, although many believe that he came from Holland. At the time of the Brussels Dog Show of 1880 this little dog was well established as a family pet and he could be seen on the barges frequenting the canals of Belgium and Holland. The Schipperke Club of England was founded in 1890 and British sportsmen who went to Belgium to hunt brought back many of these grand little dogs.

A small cobby dog, with a very sharp expression, and intensely lively. Head is foxy in appearance and his eyes should be dark brown. Ears are carried stiffly erect. Coat is abundant, dense and harsh, smooth on the head, ears and legs, but thick round the neck forming a mane and frill. Colour should be black, but other whole colours are allowed. The Schipperke is born tailless. Height: 12–13 in (30·5 cm–33 cm). Weight: 12–16 lb (5·5–7·5 kg).

Schnauzer (Standard)

This variety of Schnauzer could really be described as the prototype of the Schnauzer family. Bred in Germany for centuries, it is thought that his origin was in the crossing of the German Poodle and the Wolf Spitz family with wire-haired Pinscher stock. Schnauzers were first exhibited in Germany in 1879 as Wire-haired Pinschers. All Schnauzers in Germany have their ears cropped, but this is not permitted in Great Britain. Like the Giant Schnauzer in conformation, in a smaller compass, he is a robust dog with a keen and alert bearing. The breed was introduced into Britain by the Duchess of Montrose.

Height: dogs 19 in (48 cm), bitches 18 in (45·5 cm).

Schnauzer (Miniature)

The Miniature Schnauzer should be a miniature form of the Schnauzer and completely free from any defects owing to the reduction in size. It was bred in Germany for over half a century, but did not come to England until about 1928. These miniatures were introduced by Mr W. H. Hancock who was the founder of most of the British stock. In America the miniatures have been bred since 1925, and in both America and Canada this breed is classified as a Terrier.

Ideal height: dogs 14 in (35 cm), bitches 13 in (33 cm). It is stressed that very small toy-like dogs are not typical.

Shar-Pei

This breed survived for over 2,000 years as a very valued member of the Chinese family but by 1971 only a few specimens were known to exist. Now it seems likely that this amiable, medium sized wrinkled dog is likely to make a comeback. Puppies are even more wrinkled than the adults and give the appearance of being completely engulfed in a coat which seems far too big for the frame. One very important feature of the breed is the bluish-black tongue which is also a feature of the Chow Chow. These two breeds may be descended from each other or they may both have a common ancestor.

The Shar-Pei's original home was believed to be in the village of Dah Let in the Kwangtung Province and the villagers and farmers in this area, lacking other entertainment, staged fights between their dogs. The Shar-Pei has a very sweet disposition and will only fight if taught to do so by its owner from puppyhood.

Colour black, red or fawn. Patches of two colours on coat are undesirable. Size: 18–22 in (45·72–50·80 cm).

Shih Tzu

Shih Tzus have come from Tibet where they lived for many centuries. The dogs were taken from Tibet to the Chinese Court in the 17th century, and found great favour. In 1930 Lady Brownrigg, an English lady living in China, found some of these dogs and imported them into England. In 1946 the English Kennel Club granted them a separate register and since then they have gradually increased in number. Some excellent specimens are seen today in the show ring. In America they are classified in the Toy Group.

The Shih Tzu is a great character, full of arrogance, very lively and with a quick brain. The English standard says that he is neither a Terrier nor a Toy dog. Coat is long and dense with a good undercoat. All colours are permissible, but a white blaze on the forehead and a white tip to the tail are highly prized. Height: not more than $10\frac{1}{2}$ in (26 cm). Weight: 10–18 lb (4·5–8 kg).

Tibetan Spaniel

The Tibetan Spaniel was found in the monasteries of Tibet. Credit must go to Sir Edward and Lady Wakefield for reintroducing the breed to England after their almost complete extinction during the Second World War. The Tibetan Spaniel Association was formed in the UK in 1958.

A charming, small dog that is gay and assertive and highly intelligent. Head is small in proportion to the body, but is carried proudly, giving an air of importance. Coat is a double one, silky in texture, with ample feathering. All colours and mixture of colours are allowed. Height: 10 in (25·5 cm). Weight: 9–15 lb (4–6·5 kg).

Tibetan Terrier

This breed, although called a Terrier, is not in fact a
true terrier as it has never been used to go to ground;
in Britain it is classified with the other Tibetan breeds
in the Utility Group. These dogs have been bred for
centuries in the monasteries of Tibet. The Tibetan
Terrier is a well-muscled, medium-sized dog and in
general appearance not unlike an Old English Sheepdog in miniature.

Its skull is of medium length, with a marked stop in
front of the eyes. Head should be well furnished with
hair. Body compact and powerful. Tail carried in a gay
curl over back. Double coated and can be white, golden,
cream, grey or smoke, black, particolour and tricolour.
Height: dogs 14–16 in (35–40 cm), bitches slightly less.

6   WORKING GROUP
Alaskan Malamute

This dog comes from north-western Alaska and is regarded as the national breed of that country. It is one of the oldest Arctic sled dogs which have proved their worth on the various Arctic and Antarctic expeditions to the Poles.

An affectionate, friendly dog and not a 'one-man' dog. A loyal, devoted companion, very fond of people and especially children who enjoy driving them to sleds. Highly esteemed in Alaska both for sporting purposes and sleigh racing. A very strong dog that is quite capable of travelling at 12 mph (19 km/h) and pulling a loaded sledge 60 miles (96 km) in 18 hours. For his work he obviously has strong bone and powerful muscles. Coat is thick and dense. Colour is usually wolf-grey, black and white, or white with dark markings on head. Height: dogs 25–28 in (64–71 cm), bitches 23–26 in (58–66 cm). Weight range: 85–125 lb (38–56 kg).

Anatolian Shepherd Dog

The Anatolian Shepherd Dog is the Turkish Shepherd Guard Dog and a very ancient breed dating back 3000 years.

A large, powerfully built dog with a short dense weatherproof coat. Head large and broad between ears which are V-shaped and pendant. Neck thick, medium length with slight dewlap. Powerful back with slightly arched loins, chest deep and broad with good tuck up. Built for speed. Tail carried low in repose, curled over back when alert.

The Anatolian makes a wonderful guard/companion, but is not suited to town life as it is a lively energetic breed that needs plenty of space and exercise. In Turkey they guard flocks from wolves and rustlers. Very intelligent and affectionate. Colour cream or fawn, various greys, black or wholly white, also tricolour. Height: 30 in (76 cm). Weight: dogs 110 lb (50 kg), bitches 100 lb (45 kg).

Australian Cattle Dog

This is a dog bred by the Australian Sheep farmers to meet their demands. It is a cross between the Smithfield, Black Bob-tailed dog, Collies from Scotland, the Dingo, Kelpie and even Dalmatian. The Cattle Dog is extremely tough and able to carry out any task however arduous. He is courageous and has a natural devotion to duty.

Broad head, only slightly curved between the ears, which should be moderate in size and pricked. Coat is short and straight, of medium texture with short dense undercoat. The tail forms a good brush. The colour should be blue or blue-mottled with or without other markings. In red speckle, the colour should be even, including the undercoat which must not be white or cream. Height: dogs 18–20 in (46–51 cm), bitches 17–19 in (43–48 cm).

Bearded Collie

This is a highly intelligent and handsome type of working cattle dog with a shaggy coat and beard. The breed has become much more popular in recent years on the show bench in Britain, although at one time it was in danger of dying out. This collie should be alert, lively, self-confident and of good temperament.

He should have a long, lean body with free and active movement. The head should be broad with a flat skull and ears set high. A fairly long foreface is required with moderate stop. Coat should be a double one with the under parts soft, furry and close. The outer coat should be harsh, strong and flat. Colour is slate grey or reddish fawn, black, all shades of grey, brown and sandy, with or without white collie markings. Height: dogs 21–22 in (53–56 cm), bitches 20–21 in (51–53 cm).

Belgian Shepherd Dog
(Groenendael)

This is the best known of the three types of Belgian
Shepherds' Dogs and takes its name from the place
with which it was associated, Groenendael. The Belgian
Kennel Club recognized Groenendaels in 1897. These
dogs were first brought to England in 1931 by Mrs
Grant Forbes. Since they are sheepdogs at heart, they
show a suspicion of strangers but are easily trained and
are excellent workers.

The head should be finely chiselled, and the skull
and muzzle should be about equal in length. The body
should be powerful without being bulky, and the
movement brisk and free. The outer coat should be
long, straight and abundant. Colour should be black or
black with limited white. Height: dogs 24–26 in (61–
66 cm), bitches 22–24 in (56–61 cm).

Belgian Shepherd Dog (Laekenois)

Like the other varieties of Belgian Shepherd Dogs the Laekenois takes its name from the village where it originated. This was a small place in the neighbourhood of Boom near Antwerp. In this area there were large bleach works; the linen was put out to bleach in the fields and the dogs guarded the fields. The Laekenois varies from the Groenendael only in coat and colour. The colour should be reddish fawn with black shading, principally on the muzzle and tail. The coat should be rough, dry, untidy looking and not curly. Any sprinkling of fluffy fine hair in locks in the rough coat is not permitted. The length of the coat should be about $2\frac{1}{4}$ in (6 cm) on all parts of the body. The tail should not be plumed. Highly intelligent and makes an excellent guard.

Belgian Shepherd Dog (Malinois)

The Belgian Malinois is a variety of the Belgian Shepherd that is known in its own country as the Chien de Berger Belge Malinois and takes its name from the town of Mechlin or Malines. This dog resembles the German Shepherd Dog but is lighter in bone and smaller in stature. The Malinois is identical to the Groenendael except for coat and colour.

The hair on the head should be very short, and this applies also to the exterior of the ears and the lower parts of the legs. It should be short on the rest of the body, thicker on the tail and around the neck, where it should resemble a ridge or collar. The hindquarters should be fringed with longer hair. Tail should be thick and bushy. Colour should be dark fawn with considerable black overlay. Black shading on muzzle and ears desirable. Height: dogs 24–26 in (61–66 cm), bitches 22–24 in (56–61 cm).

Belgian Shepherd Dog (Tervueren)

Like the other Belgian Shepherd Dog breeds the Tervueren has been named from the town where it originated. This dog is not as well known as the Groenendael, but as the two were given separate breed status in 1959, the Tervueren has made good progress, both in the UK and in the USA.

This breed is very similar to the Groenendael apart from the colour which may include all shades of red, fawn and grey with black overlay (that is, the tip of each hair should be blackened). On mature males this blackening should be especially pronounced on the shoulders, back and rib section. The face should have a black mask and the ears should be mostly black. After 18 months the Tervueren's colour should be set and, if too black and resembling a Groenendael, then it is a fault. Size is the same as the Groenendael.

Bernese Mountain Dog

This dog originates in Switzerland and is a very handsome dog. There are nearly 200 of them in Britain and the quality and type has steadily increased. One of the four varieties of Swiss Mountain Dogs, it is aristocratic in appearance and about the size of a Collie with a long coat, small drop ears and a long bushy tail. These dogs were used as draught dogs in their own country, but today they are more valued as companions and watchdogs for homes.

Their colour is jet black with russet-brown or deep tan markings on all four legs. There should be a spot just above the forelegs, markings each side of the white chest, and spots over the eyes should always be seen. The brown on the forelegs must always be between the black and white. The coat should be soft and silky with bright natural sheen. Height: dogs 26–27 in (66–68 cm), bitches 24–26 in (61–66 cm).

The Border Collie

The Border Collie is one of the world's finest sheepdogs and has been used for centuries to herd the sheep. Originally he was known as the Shepherds' Dog, the English Collie, the Working Collie and finally the Border Collie. The Border has just recently been recognized by the English Kennel Club and separate classes are now given at dog shows. Sheepdog trials have been held since 1873 in Wales.

The head is essentially an old-fashioned Collie head, fairly broad in skull, slightly blunt in muzzle. Expression bold and keen in action, soft and appealing when at rest. Coat very dense and of varied lengths. Colour black, grey or blue merle with white points. It can be black/white/tan. Height: dogs 18 in (45·5 cm), bitches 17 in (43 cm).

Bouvier des Flandres

This dog is a descendant of the Belgian Cattle Dogs and its popularity has spread to many parts of Europe, Canada and the USA. A large, coarse-haired, prick-eared dog with a very conspicuous head and short docked tail. The Bouvier was first shown in Brussels in 1910, and the standard was drawn up in 1912 and revised in 1926.

This dog is used in country areas as a drover and cattle dog, and it is true to say that the breeders in its homeland are anxious to keep its working abilities. The Bouvier is a compact, powerfully built dog of upstanding carriage with an alert and intelligent expression. The coat is rough and capable of withstanding the hardest work in the worst weather. The colour goes from fawn to black, pepper and salt, grey and brindle. Height: dogs $23\frac{1}{2}$–$27\frac{1}{2}$ in (59–69 cm), bitches $22\frac{3}{4}$–$25\frac{1}{2}$ in (58–64 cm).

Boxer

The Boxer is one of the most popular working breeds. His character is of the greatest importance as he has always been renowned for his great loyalty to his master and is an ardent protector of his own family. In 1896 the German Boxer Club was formed with the object of stabilizing the breed, but it was not until 1905 that the German fanciers could agree on a standard.

The head imparts to the Boxer a unique individual stamp. The Boxer is of moderate size, full of energy and very strong. American and some Continental Boxers are cropped, but in the UK they are left natural. The coat should be short and glossy, lying smooth and tight to the body. The permissible colours are fawn, brindle and fawn in various shades from light yellow to deer red. White markings are allowed and a black mask is essential. Height: dogs 22–24 in (56–61 cm), bitches 21–23 in (53–58 cm).

Briard

This dog comes from a very old race of sheepdogs from the Brie district in France. An official standard was approved in France in 1925 and revised in 1930.

The Briard is a dog of rugged appearance, supple, muscular and well proportioned, gay and lively. His head is strong and fairly long, with a well-defined stop placed exactly mid-way. A ,moustache, beard and eyebrows are characteristics of the breed. This is one of the few breeds that require back dew claws to be left on. The dog should cover a great deal of ground on the move. Coat must be not less than 3 in (7 cm) on the body—slightly wavy and very dry. All solid colours are correct except white, chestnut, mahogany and bi-colour. Height: dogs 23–27 in (58·5–68·5 cm), bitches 22–25½ in (55·5–64·5 cm).

Bullmastiff

The Bullmastiff did not gain recognition until 1924 when a Breed Club was formed. The Kennel Club accepted registrations with the proviso that only dogs with at least three generations of pure-bred Bullmastiff be registered. Previously Mastiffs had been crossed with Bulldogs to produce the breed. In 1933 the American Kennel Club granted recognition.

The temperament of the Bullmastiff combines high spirits, reliability, activity, endurance and alertness. The skull should be large and square with fair wrinkle when interested. He should not appear cumbersome although he is a very powerfully built dog. Back should be short and straight giving a compact carriage. Coat is short and hard. Any shade of brindle, fawn or red is permissible, but the colour must be pure and clear. Height: dogs 25–27 in (63–68 cm), bitches 24–26 in (61–66 cm). Weight: dogs 110–130 lb (50–59 kg), bitches 90–110 lb (41–50 kg).

Collie (Rough)

Very often the Collie is called the Scotch Collie, but as all Collies originated from Scotland, this is superfluous. The Collie was originally a very robust sheepdog and an expert at handling large flocks, but in recent years the breed has become more streamlined and elegant in appearance. The modern Collie was first shown at Birmingham in 1860.

These dogs are most handsome, and their eyes and ears give the true expression of the Collie. Their ears are very mobile and expressive, and are set not too close together on the top of the skull. The body should be a trifle long compared to the height. Movement is a distinct characteristic of this breed as it moves with its front feet comparatively close together. Coat should fit the outline of the dog and be very dense. There are three recognized colours: sable and white, tricolour and blue merle. Height: 22–24 in (56–61 cm), bitches 20–22 in (51–56 cm).

Collie (Smooth)

The Smooth-haired Collie is not nearly so numerous in numbers as his long-coated friend. This variety first had classes at Darlington Show in 1870, but it is interesting to note that at the first Club Show for the breed in 1885, the catalogue states that roughs and smooths were coming from the same breeding. The Smooth Collie is identical to the Rough variety apart from the coat, which is a very important feature of the Smooth Collie. The coat should have a harsh texture with a very dense undercoat.

The three recognized colours are sable and white, tricolour and blue merle; with this colour one often finds one or both eyes 'wall' or jewelled. Proportionately there seem to be more merle colours in the smooth varieties than in the roughs. The size is the same as in the Rough Collie.

Dobermann

This German breed is a manufactured breed whose origins are well known. It took its name from Louis Dobermann who, by 1890, had bred a good type of Pinscher. Following this Otto Galler improved the breed and added Pinscher to the name. Since the turn of the century no crosses have been introduced, and since 1922 breeding in Germany has been very carefully controlled. The National Dobermann Club in Germany was formed in 1900.

The Dobermann is a streamlined dog full of power, agility and elegance. He has a proud carriage and a bold, alert temperament. The head should be long, well filled under the eyes and clean cut. The Dobermann is an unsurpassed watchdog and very loyal to his family. His coat is smooth, short, hard, thick and close lying. Colours allowed are definite black, brown or blue with rust red markings. Height: dogs 27 in (69·5 cm), bitches 25½ in (64 cm).

Estrela Mountain Dog

The Estrela Mountain Dog is known in its homeland as the Cao Serra da Estrela. It is one of the oldest breeds of the Iberian peninsula. A sturdy well built dog of mastiff type covering an impression of strength and vigour.

. Head is long and powerful with a broad, slightly rounded skull. Eyes of medium size and oval in shape with a lovely calm expression. Ears are small in relation to the body. Back horizontal and preferably short. Chest deep, broad and well sprung without being barrel. Thighs well muscled. Gait is strong with plenty of drive. Tail should reach to hock when animal is standing. Coat short, thick moderately harsh and straight with a short dense undercoat. Colour should be any colour varying from burnt yellow through reddish gold to deep red, and wolf colour. A black muzzle is highly desirable.

Height: $25\frac{1}{2}$–$28\frac{1}{2}$ in (65–72 cm) for dogs, $24\frac{1}{2}$–27 in (62–68 cm) for bitches.

German Shepherd Dog
(Alsatian)

The Alsatian first attracted attention in 1882 at Hanover Show. During the two world wars about 25,000 dogs of this breed lost their lives in the service of man. This dog is derived from the old breeds of herding and farm dogs. Above medium size, long bodied and very muscular, with a steady gait enabling him to cover the maximum amount of ground with a minimum expenditure of energy. Head is long, lean and clean cut, broad at back of skull, only a slight stop between eyes, muzzle strong and long with powerful jaws. May be of any colour but white is undesirable. Coat should be a double coat of medium length.

This dog is distinguished for loyalty and courage, and used by the Police, the Services and as a Guide Dog for the Blind. The English Kennel Club agreed in 1977 that this breed should be known in Britain as The German Shepherd Dog (Alsatian). Height: dogs 24–26 in (61–66 cm), bitches 22–24 in (56–61 cm).

Great Dane

The Great Dane is known in Germany as the Deutsche Dogge or German Mastiff. Around the 17th century the German nobility used these dogs to hunt boars and stags. Today they are much more elegant and refined than their ancestors. In 1883 a breed club was formed in Great Britain known as the Great Dane Club and this club still exists today.

The Great Dane should be remarkable in size and very muscular. Elegance of outline and grace of form are most essential to a Dane, who has a charming temperament. An alert and fearless guard and, when space is available, he makes a very intelligent house dog and companion. Coat is short, dense and sleek looking. Colours are brindle, fawn, black, blue and harlequin, which must have a pure white underground with black or blue patches. Height: dogs minimum 30 in (76 cm), bitches 28 in (71 cm). Minimum weight: dogs 120 lb (54 kg), bitches 100 lb (45 kg).

Hovawart

The Hovawart was re-created by German breeders
from farmers' dogs of the Hartz, Black Forest and other
mountain regions and was given official recognition in
Germany in 1936.

A medium sized active, alert, long coated dog with
drop ears and bushy tail. Head is broad and domed.
Skull about equal in length to the muzzle which is
powerful and blunt. Cheeks narrow. Jaws strong. Back
firm, straight and strong. Loins broad and arched.
Chest deep and broad but not barrel-shaped. Tail long,
thick at the root and tapering to the tip, well feathered.
Coat waved but lying flat without curl. Colour deep
golden, black and gold or black (not dark brown)
without white markings except for a few white hairs at
the tip of tail.

The Hovawart is a very intelligent, alert and easily
trained guard and companion dog.

Height: for dogs 25–27 in (63–68 cm), for bitches 22–
26 in (55–66 cm).

Hungarian Puli

This breed is probably the best known Hungarian breed outside its own country. The first standard was drawn up in Hungary in 1915, but was revised in 1924 and again in 1955. Used in his homeland as a herder and drover, he has done this job for over 1200 years. The first Puli arrived in England about 1950 when he was shown at a Midlands Show. The Hungarian Puli Club of Great Britain was officially approved by the Kennel Club at the end of 1971.

The Puli's coat is unique in the canine world, hanging in tight cords which can reach the ground when the dog is mature. A medium-sized, nimble and extremely intelligent dog, his head should be fine and round with a slightly domed skull. The Puli is a short striding dog, always nimble, quick and gay. Acceptable coat colours are black, rusty black, various shades of grey and white. Height: 16–18 in (41–46 cm), bitches 14–16 in (36–41 cm).

Husky (Eskimo Dog)

This Husky probably originated in Eastern Siberia but has for many years lived in Greenland, Labrador, Northern Canada and Alaska. In general shape and make he shows a great resemblance to the Siberian Husky, the Alaskan Malamute and the Samoyed. Like these other breeds he has great strength and endurance, and in his homeland pulls a sledge in the winter. In the summer he helps pull the fishing boats ashore.

Top coat is thick from 3 to 5 in (7–12·5 cm) and the undercoat is soft. Colour black, white, black and white, wolf to blue-grey, tan or reddish-fawn and any combination of these colours. He is naturally suspicious of strangers and a very excellent guard dog. Does not bark but howls more like a wolf. Height: dogs 22–25 in (56–65·3 cm), bitches 20–22 in (51–56 cm). Weight: dogs 70–92 lb (32–42 kg), bitches 53–75 lb (24–34 kg).

Husky (Siberian)

This Husky came from North-East Asia and was used as an endurance sled dog by the Chukchi people. These dogs had to be capable of travelling great distances at a moderate speed and carrying a load in low temperatures. They are the ancestors of the breed known today as the Siberian Husky. They are extremely gentle and friendly in disposition, and may be readily trained for almost any kind of work.

These Huskies are versatile dogs of great beauty and are quick and light on the feet which are slightly webbed. The moderately compact body, which is well-furred, erect ears and brush tail all suggest their Northern heritage. Gait is smooth and seemingly effortless. Tail is well-furred or round fox brush shape and should usually be carried over back in a graceful sickle curve. Coat is double and all colours including white are allowed plus all markings. Height: dogs 21–23½ in (53–59 cm), bitches 20–22 in (51–56 cm). Weight: dogs 45–60 lb (20–27 kg), bitches 35–50 lb (16–23 kg).

Komondor

The Komondor is the largest of the Hungarian herdsman's dogs and is of Asiatic origin; it is an excellent guard, wary of strangers, courageous and devoted to his master. He will defend against any attack and because of this was more generally used as a guard dog rather than for driving herds.

He is a large muscular dog with plenty of bone and is particularly noted for his strength and courageous manner. His coat is one of his characteristics as the hair should tend to cling together like tassels, giving a corded appearance, even when combed. The coat is fairly slow in cording and may not be fully formed before the dog is two years old. The puppy coat should be soft and fluffy. This dog is always white and ideally the skin should be grey. Height: dogs 26–31½ in (66–79 cm), bitches 23½–27½ in (59–70 cm). Weight: dogs 110–135 lb (50–61 kg), bitches 80–110 lb (36–50 kg).

Lancashire Heeler

This is a low-set, small but strong and active worker. Very happy when working cattle in a manner expected of a heeler but with his strong terrier characteristics he is also happy hunting rabbits or exterminating rats.

The skull is flat and wide between the ears, tapering gradually towards the eyes which are set wide apart. These should be dark and almond shaped. Ears to show an alert lift or to be erect. Body must have well sprung ribs which extend well back. Tail should be set-on high, must not be docked but carried over the back when the dog is alert. Coat not to be too long or stand-offish and the colour to be black with deep mahogany tan markings on the muzzle with spots on the cheeks and often over the eyes. A desirable thumb-mark immediately above the feet, inside the hindlegs and under the tail. The preferred colour should not include any white. This breed is always ready to protect the home or car when it is given the opportunity.

Height: 12 in (30·48 cm) for dogs and 10 in (25·40 cm) for bitches.

Maremma Sheepdog

This is the best known of the Italian Sheepdogs and has been called various names, the most common being Cane de Pastore Maremmani, or Abruzzes Maremma The present line of Maremmas in England first started in 1932 when Count Chigi sent to Mrs Helen Home-Robertson and her sister Mrs J. M. Pryor, Drago of Castlenuova. A few years later a bitch was given to Mrs Home-Robertson as a mate for Drago. In 1936 the first litter of Maremmas whelped in England and in 1950 the breed had a separate breed class at Crufts.

The Italian Sheepdog is a large dog of majestic appearance. He is sturdy and courageous without being at all aggressive. The body is strong with well-developed muscles. The coat should fit the outline of the dog and be long, plentiful and rather harsh. A slight waviness is permitted, but never a curly coat The colour of the coat should be white, ivory, or pale fawn, with or without slightly darker shading. A minimum size of $25\frac{1}{2}$ in (64 cm) for a dog and $23\frac{1}{2}$ in (59 cm) for a bitch.

Mastiff

The history of the Mastiff goes back to centuries BC. This breed has been changed from a fierce fighting breed into a calm guard and charming companion. In 1908, 35 Mastiffs were registered at the English Kennel Club, but the 1939–40 war took a great toll of their numbers and several breeders sent their stock to America. Only three litters were born during the war, and when peace returned to Britain there were only about 20 Mastiffs in the country, many of them too old to breed from. To save the Mastiff from extinction, the Old English Mastiff Club bought back stock from America.

The Mastiff is a large, massive, powerful dog with a combination of grandeur and good nature, plus courage and docility. He has a heavy head and a short close-lying coat. The colours can be apricot or silver, fawn or dark fawn-brindle. Muzzle, ears and nose should be black. Minimum height dogs: 30 in (76 cm), bitches from $27\frac{1}{2}$ in (69 cm).

Newfoundland

How the Newfoundland arrived in Newfoundland nobody seems to know. The standardization of the breed took place in England in the 19th century and six of this breed were shown at Birmingham in 1860. The English Kennel Club accepted them on their register in 1878. This is a strong and massive breed that loves the water and they have been used for lifesaving. Exceptionally gentle and docile dogs.

The bone on this dog is massive throughout, but he should move freely on his legs with his body swung loosely between them. Head should be broad and massive. Eyes are small and of a dark brown colour. Coat should be flat and dense, and rather coarse in texture. Colour should be dull jet black, brown or white with black markings which are known as Landseers. Height: dogs 28 in (71 cm), bitches 26 in (66 cm).

Norwegian Buhund

This breed has been kept as a farm dog in the Norwegian countryside for thousands of years, but it was only as recently as 1943 that it was officially recognized.

The Buhund is a medium-sized Spitz dog with erect ears and short curled tail. He first arrived in England in 1946 and is steadily claiming his own popularity. His top coat is long, thick and harsh. On the head and front of the limbs the hair should be short and smooth, but longer on the chest, neck and shoulders and behind the thighs. Colour is wheaten, black or not too dark red and wolf sable, all preferably self-coloured. Dogs not more than 17¾ in (45 cm), bitches somewhat less.

Old English Sheepdog

It seems likely that the breed was first developed in the West Country of England, but from which breeds it was produced is a matter of conjecture. A strong, compact dog of great symmetry, absolutely free from legginess and profusely coated all over. Commonly known as the Bobtail, this dog has a charming character and makes an excellent guard.

This Sheepdog is very elastic in gallop, but in walking or trotting has a characteristic ambling or pacing movement. Skull is capacious and rather squarely formed giving room for brain power. The stop must be defined thus avoiding a Deerhound appearance. Eyes are dark or 'wall'-eyed. Coat is profuse and of good hard texture; not straight but shaggy and free from curl. Any shade of grey, grizzle, blue or blue merle, with or without white markings. Any shade of brown or sable is objectionable. Height: dogs 22 in (56 cm) and upwards. Slightly less for bitches. A long narrow head is a serious fault.

Pinscher

This is a very old established German breed mentioned in the very earliest writings and officially recognised in 1879. Since 1895 it has been fostered in Germany by the Pinscher-Schnauzer Club. A medium sized short haired, actively built dog with bold head carriage and either erect or drop ears. Head of medium length with slightly domed skull. Scissor bite. Back short and strong with loins slightly tucked up. Tail set on high and docked. Feet small, round and pointing straight forward. Colour black with red or golden tan points— dark brown, either whole coloured or with tan markings. Markings as clear as possible. The Pinscher is a very intelligent and lively companion and excellent watchdog, suspicious of strangers. Makes a very good ratter. Height: about 18 in (45 cm).

Pyrenean Mountain Dog

This is a most impressive breed which has come from the Pyrenees. Here they were used as natural guard dogs and protectors of the shepherds and their flocks. An immensely strong yet well-balanced dog of great size. Head is most attractive and gives the impression of strength with no sign of coarseness. The expression should be intelligent and contemplative. His gait should be unhurried and one should get the impression of a large dog being propelled by powerful hindquarters. Coat should consist of an undercoat that is profuse and composed of fine hairs, while the outer coat should be coarse in texture, thick and straight, or slightly wavy but never curly.

The colour is mainly white with patches of badger, wolf grey or pale yellow or white only. Height: dogs 28 in (71 cm), bitches 26 in (66 cm). Great size should be regarded as absolutely essential, provided type and character are retained.

Rottweiler

Originally the Rottweiler was created by cattle dealers in the Swabian town of Rottweil, but in the last century breeders have developed its guarding instincts and the Rottweiler is now recognized as one of Germany's foremost working breeds. The Rottweiler is both bold and loyal, and is unexcelled as a guard. This dog first came to England in 1936, and in 1966 was granted a separate register.

The Rottweiler is an above average sized stalwart dog. His tranquil gaze manifests good nature and devotion. The chest should be roomy, broad and deep with the ribs well sprung. In movement the Rottweiler should convey an impression of supple strength and endurance. The top coat should be of medium length, coarse and flat. The undercoat should not show throught the outer coat. The colour is black with clearly defined markings on the cheeks, muzzle, chest and legs, as well as over both eyes and beneath the tail. Height: dogs 25–27 in (63·5–68·5 cm), bitches 23–25 in (58·5–63·5 cm).

Schnauzer (Giant)

The Giant variety of Schnauzer is more rare in Britain than its smaller brothers and sisters, but there are over 150 of this breed registered at the English Kennel Club. In Munich, in October 1909, about thirty black dogs were shown as Russian Bear Schnauzers. These had been bred in the Bavarian Highlands by the farmers and cattle dealers. In Germany, in 1925, the breed was classified as a working dog.

The head is long and powerful with a stubby moustache and whiskers. A strong body that is nearly square. His temperament combines high spirits, reliability, strength, endurance and vigour. Colour is pepper and salt with colours in even proportions or pure black. Coat is hard and wiry, and just short enough for smartness. A good undercoat is essential. Height: dogs $25\frac{1}{2}$–$27\frac{1}{2}$ (64–69 cm), bitches $23\frac{1}{2}$–$25\frac{1}{2}$ in (59–64 cm).

St Bernard

This breed has been known for a century as the Good Samaritan Dog as he has been responsible for rescuing many lost wayfarers in the Swiss Alps. The dogs of the Bernadine Hospice were world famous for their many marvellous deeds in helping humans. Dogs were first bred at the Bernadine Hospice between 1660 and 1670. The name St Bernard first came into use in England in 1865. A Breed Club was formed in London in 1880 and held its first show two years later.

The St Bernard is a very large, powerful dog with a smooth or long coat, massive head, pendant ears; his expression should betoken benevolence, dignity and intelligence. The colour can be orange-brindle, mahogany-brindle, red-brindle, white with patches on body of any of the above named colours. The general outline should suggest great power and capability of endurance and, as regards height, the taller the better.

Samoyed

One of the most beautiful members of the Spitz family.
For centuries, this dog has served the Siberian tribe
after which he is named—the Samoyedes—as a hard-
working sleigh dog. In addition he herds the reindeer
and guards his master's property. The first Samoyeds
came to Britain about 1900 with fur traders. The
Samoyed is sometimes called the smiling dog. The
Samoyed Club was formed in 1909, and the breed has
made great progress since then.

Essentially a working dog, he should be strong,
active and graceful. He has a thick, close, soft and short
undercoat, with harsh hair growing through it to form
the outer coat, which should stand straight away from
the body and be free from curl. Colour is pure white,
white and biscuit, cream. Height: dogs 20–22 in (51–
56 cm), bitches 18–20 in (46–51 cm).

Shetland Sheepdog

As its name implies, this dog comes from the Shetland Islands off the north coast of Scotland. The Shetland Sheepdog Club was formed at Lerwick in 1908 with the aim of encouraging the breeding of these small collies and in 1910 it set up the first full standard of the breed. At the same time this club changed the name from Shetland Collie to Shetland Sheepdog.

The Sheltie appeals as a dog of great beauty, intelligence and alertness. An abundance of coat, mane and frill, with shapeliness of head and sweetness of expression all combine to present the ideal Shetland Sheepdog that will secure admiration. The action of the Shetland Sheepdog should denote speed and smoothness. Coat must be double. Outer coat of long harsh texture and undercoat soft, short and close. The colours are tricolour, sable, blue merle, black and tan, and black and white. Height: dogs 14½ in (36 cm), pitches 14 in (35·5 cm).

Vastgotaspets
(Swedish Vallhund)

A small, powerful and low to ground dog with a fairly long back. An old established herder used by the Swedish farmers, it was accepted by the Swedish Kennel Club as a pure breed on the 20th October 1943. The Vallhund and the Welsh Corgi are distantly related.

The head should be rather long and clean cut with an almost flat skull and well-defined stop. There are now quite a number of the breed in this country. Coat medium short, with harsh, close and tight top-coat and an abundant soft and woolly undercoat. Desirable colours are steel-grey, greyish-brown, greyish-yellow, reddish-yellow or reddish-brown with darker hairs on the back, neck and sides of body. Height: dogs 13 in (33 cm), bitches 12·3 in (31 cm).

Welsh Corgi (Cardigan)

The Cardigan Welsh Corgi is one of the oldest breeds in the UK, but he has become a show dog only in recent years. These dogs have been most useful to the Welsh farmers for centuries, but it was not until 1925 that they appeared at dog shows for the first time. The Cardigan was shown with the Pembroke as one breed, but in 1934 the English Kennel Club classified them separately.

The Cardigan's head should be as foxy in expression as possible. His body should measure about 36 in (91·5 cm) from point of nose to tip of tail. Coat is short and of hard texture. Tail is moderately long and set in line with body, but not curled over back. Any colour is permitted except pure white. Height: 12 in (30 cm). Weight: dogs 22–26 lb (10–12 kg), bitches 20–24 lb (9–11 kg).

Welsh Corgi (Pembroke)

The Pembrokes were, like the Cardigans, essentially cattle drivers and have been used as such in Wales for centuries. It is said to have been a dwarf dog brought to England by Flemish weavers about the year 1100. Some of the weavers moved to the south-west corner of Wales and crossed their dogs with the native dog. This applied particularly in Pembrokeshire. Cardigans and Pembrokeshire Corgis were interbred very early in this century, but since the English Kennel Club gave separate classification in 1934 this has been stopped. The Pembroke Corgi has always been a great favourite with Her Majesty the Queen, and this no doubt has helped the breed's tremendous rise in popularity.

A low-set sturdy dog with a short tail which is preferably natural. Coat of medium length and not wiry. Self colours in red, sable, fawn, black and tan, or with white markings. Height: 10–12 in (25–30 cm). Weight: dogs 20–24 lb (9–11 kg), bitches 18–22 lb (8–10 kg).

Top Thirty Breeds Registered at the Kennel Club 1982

Breed	*No. of Registrations*
German Shepherd Dogs (Alsatians)	18,124
Labrador Retrievers	13,488
Yorkshire Terriers	12,755
Golden Retrievers	9,702
Cavalier King Charles Spaniels	9,539
Cocker Spaniels	7,697
English Springer Spaniels	6,984
Dobermanns	6,244
Collies (Rough)	5,663
Boxers	4,077
Staffordshire Bull Terriers	3,968
Shetland Sheepdogs	3,808
West Highland White Terriers	3,485
Poodles (Toy)	3,100
Old English Sheepdogs	2,807
Irish Setters	2,675
Rottweilers	2,466
Cairn Terriers	2,384
Pekingese	2,277
Great Danes	2,255
Chihuahuas (Longcoat)	1,857
Bull Terriers	1,626
Dachshunds (Miniature Long-haired)	1,618
Poodles (Miniature)	1,538
Shih Tzus	1,397
Airedale Terriers	1,327
Welsh Corgis (Pembroke)	1,320
Border Terriers	1,291
Whippets	1,247
Bearded Collies	1,179

List of Breeds, in Groups, Granted Championship Show Status by the English Kennel Club

Gundog Group

English Setter
German Shorthaired
    Pointer
German Wirehaired Pointer
Gordon Setter
Hungarian Vizsla
Irish Setter
Large Munsterlander
Pointer
Retriever (Curly Coated)
Retriever (Flat Coated)
Retriever (Golden)
Retriever (Labrador)
Spaniel (American Cocker)
Spaniel (Clumber)
Spaniel (Cocker)
Spaniel (English Springer)
Spaniel (Field)
Spaniel (Irish Water)
Spaniel (Sussex)
Spaniel (Welsh Springer)
Weimaraner

Hound Group

Afghan Hound
Basenji
Bassett Griffon Vendeen
Basset Hound
Beagle
Bloodhound
Borzoi
Dachshund (Long-haired)
Dachshund (Smooth-
    haired)
Dachshund (Wire-haired)
Dachshund (Miniature
    Long-haired)
Dachshund (Miniature
    Smooth-haired)
Dachshund (Miniature
    Wire-haired)
Deerhound
Elkhound
Finnish Spitz
Greyhound
Ibizan Hound
Irish Wolfhound
Pharaoh Hound
Rhodesian Ridgeback
Saluki or Gazelle Hound
Whippet

Terrier Group

Airedale Terrier
Australian Terrier
Bedlington Terrier
Border Terrier
Bull Terrier
Bull Terrier (Miniature)
Cairn Terrier
Dandie Dinmont Terrier
Fox Terrier (Smooth)
Fox Terrier (Wire)
Irish Terrier
Kerry Blue Terrier
Lakeland Terrier
Manchester Terrier
Norfolk Terrier
Norwich Terrier
Scottish Terrier
Sealyham Terrier
Skye Terrier
Soft-coated Wheaten
    Terrier
Staffordshire Bull Terrier

Welsh Terrier
West Highland White
  Terrier

Toy Group

Bichon Frise
Cavalier King Charles
  Spaniel
Chihuahua (Long Coat)
Chihauhua (Smooth Coat)
Chinese Crested Dog
English Toy Terrier (Black
  and Tan)
Griffon Bruxellois
Italian Greyhound
Japanese Chin
King Charles Spaniel
Lowchen
Maltese
Miniature Pinscher
Papillon
Pekingese
Pomeranian
Pug
Yorkshire Terrier

Utility Group

Boston Terrier
Bulldog
Chow Chow
Dalmatian
French Bulldog
Keeshond
Lhasa Apso
Poodle (Standard)
Poodle (Miniature)
Poodle (Toy)
Schipperke

Schnauzer (Miniature)
Schnauzer (Standard)
Shih Tzu
Tibetan Spaniel
Tibetan Terrier

Working Group

Bearded Collie
Belgian Shepherd Dog
  (Groenendael)
Belgian Shepherd Dog
  (Tervueren)
Bernese Mountain Dog
Border Collie
Boxer
Briard
Bullmastiff
Collie (Rough)
Collie (Smooth)
Dobermann
German Shepherd Dog
  (Alsatian)
Great Dane
Hungarian Puli
Maremma Sheepdog
Mastiff
Newfoundland
Norwegian Buhund
Old English Sheepdog
Pyrenean Mountain Dog
Rottweiler
Schnauzer (Giant)
St Bernard
Samoyed
Shetland Sheepdog
Siberian Husky
Swedish Vallhund
Welsh Corgi (Cardigan)
Welsh Corgi (Pembroke)

List of Breeds, in Groups, as Accepted by the American Kennel Club

Group I
Sporting Dogs

Pointer
Pointer, German Short-
    haired
Pointer, German Wire-
    haired
Retriever, Chesapeake Bay
Retriever, Curly-coated
Retriever, Flat-coated
Retriever, Golden
Retriever, Labrador
Setter, English
Setter, Gordon
Setter, Irish
Spaniel, American Water
Spaniel, Brittany
Spaniel, Clumber
Spaniel, Cocker
Spaniel, English Cocker
Spaniel, English Springer
Spaniel, Field
Spaniel, Irish Water
Spaniel, Sussex
Spaniel, Welsh Springer
Vizsla
Weimaraner
Wire-haired Pointing
    Griffon

Group II Hounds

Afghan Hound
Basenji
Basset Hound
Beagle
Black and Tan Coonhound
Bloodhound
Borzoi
Dachshund

Foxhound, American
Foxhound, English
Greyhound
Harrier
Irish Wolfhound
Norwegian Elkhound
Otterhound
Rhodesian Ridgeback
Saluki
Scottish Deerhound
Whippet

Group III Working Dogs

Alaskan Malamute
Belgian Malinois
Belgian Sheepdog
Belgian Tervueren
Bernese Mountain Dog
Bouvier des Flandres
Boxer
Briard
Bullmastiff
Collie
Dobermann Pinscher
German Shepherd Dog
Giant Schnauzer
Great Dane
Great Pyrenees
Komondor
Kuvasz
Mastiff
Newfoundland
Old English Sheepdog
Puli
Rottweiler
St Bernard
Samoyed
Shetland Sheepdog

Siberian Husky
Standard Schnauzer
Welsh Corgi, Cardigan
Welsh Corgi, Pembroke

Group IV Terriers

Airedale Terrier
American Staffordshire
  Terrier
Australian Terrier
Bedlington Terrier
Border Terrier
Bull Terrier
Cairn Terrier
Dandie Dinmont Terrier
Fox Terrier
Irish Terrier
Kerry Blue Terrier
Lakeland Terrier
Manchester Terrier
Miniature Schnauzer
Norwich Terrier
Scottish Terrier
Sealyham Terrier
Skye Terrier
Welsh Terrier
West Highland White
  Terrier

Group V Toys

Affenpinscher
Brussels Griffon
Chihuahua
English Toy Spaniel
Italian Greyhound
Japanese Spaniel
Maltese
Manchester Terrier (Toy)
Miniature Pinscher
Papillon
Pekingese
Pomeranian
Poodle (Toy)
Pug
Shih Tzu
Silky Terrier
Yorkshire Terrier

Group VI Non-
  sporting Dogs

Boston Terrier
Bulldog
Chow Chow
Dalmatian
French Bulldog
Keeshond
Lhasa Apso
Poodle
Schipperke

Winners of award for 'Best in Show' at Crufts 1936–1991

Year	Dog's Name	Breed	Sex	Owner	Breeder
1936	Ch. Choonam Hung Kwong	Chow Chow	D	Mrs Mannooch	Owner
1937	Ch. Cheverells Ben of Banchory	Labrador Retriever	D	Lorna, Countess Howe	Mr R. G. Heaton
1938	Exquisite Model of Ware	Cocker Spaniel	B	Mr H. S. Lloyd	Mr C. C. D. Youings
1939	Exquisite Model of Ware	Cocker Spaniel	B	Mr H. S. Lloyd	Mr C. C. D. Youings
1940–1947	Not held				
1948	Tracey Witch of Ware	Cocker Spaniel	B	Mr H. S. Lloyd	Miss D. Weldon
1949	Not held				
1950	Tracey Witch of Ware	Cocker Spaniel	B	Mr H. S. Lloyd	Miss D. Weldon
1951	Ch. Twynstar Dyma-Fi	Welsh Terrier	B	Capt. and Mrs Thomas	Mr T. M. Jones
1952	Ch. Noways-Chuckles	Bulldog	B	Mr J. Barnard	Owner
1953	Ch. Elch Edler of Ouborough	Great Dane	D	Mr W. G. Siggers	Mr J. V. Rank
1954	Not held				

176

Year	Dog's Name	Breed	Sex	Owner	Breeder
1955	Ch. Tzigane Aggri of Nashend	Poodle	D	Mrs Proctor	Owner
1956	Ch. Treetops Golden Falcon	Greyhound	D	Mrs de Casembroot and Miss H. Greenish	Owners
1957	Ch. Volkrijk of Vorden	Keeshond	B	Mrs I. Tucker	Owner
1958	Ch. Chiming Bells	Pointer	B	Mrs Parkinson	Mrs M. Bowman
1959	Ch. Sandstorm-Saracen	Welsh Terrier	D	Mrs M. M. Thomas and Mrs D. M. Leach	Mrs E. M. Russell
1960	Ch. Sulhampstead Merman	Irish Wolfhound	D	Mrs F. Nagle and Miss M. Clarke	Owners
1961	Ch. Riverina Tweedsbairn	Airedale Terrier	D	Miss P. McCaughey and Mrs D. Schuth	Mrs C. M. Halford
1962	Ch. Crackwyn Cockspur	Fox Terrier (Wire)	D	Mr H. L. Gill	Owner
1963	Ch. Rogerholme Recruit	Lakeland Terrier	D	Mr B Rogers	Major Horseman
1964	Sh. Ch. Silbury Soames of Madavale	English Setter	D	Mrs A. W. Williams	Mr and Mrs-Gardiner-Swann
1965	Ch. Fenton of Kent-wood	Alsatian (G.S.D.)	D	Miss S. H. Godden	Owner
1966	Ch. Oakington Puckshill Amber Sunblush	Poodle (Toy)	B	Mrs C. E. Perry	Mrs Dobson

177

Year	Dog's Name	Breed	Sex	Owner	Breeder
1967	Ch. Stingray of Derryabah	Lakeland Terrier	D	Mr and Mrs Postlethwaite	Owners
1968	Ch. Fanhill Faune	Dalmatian	B	Mrs E. J. Woodyatt	Owner
1969	Hendrawen's Nibelung of Charavigne	Alsatian (G.S.D.)	D	Mr and Mrs E. J. White	Mrs I. Dummett
1970	Bergerie Knur	Pyrenean Mountain Dog	D	Mr and Mrs F. S. Prince	Miss P. M. Grant-Dalton
1971	Ramacon Swash-buckler	Alsatian (G.S.D.)	D	Prince Ahmed Husain	Mr W. Rankin
1972	Ch. Abraxas-Audacity	Bull Terrier	D	Miss V. Drummond-Dick	Owner
1973	Ch. Alansmere Aquarius	Cavalier King Charles Spaniel	D	Mr Hall and Mr Evans	Owners
1974	Ch. Burtonswood Bossy Boots	St Bernard	D	Miss M. Hindes	Owner
1975	Ch. Brooke-Wire Brandy of Layven	Wire Fox Terrier	B	Messrs Benelli and Dondina	F. Robinson
1976	Ch. Dianthus Burton	West Highland White Terrier	D	Mrs K. Newstead and Mrs D. Taylor	Owners
1977	Ch. Bournehouse Dancing Master	English Setter	D	Mr G. F. Williams	Owner
1978	Ch. Harrowhill Huntsman	Wire Fox Terrier	D	Miss E. Howles	Owner

Year	Dog's Name	Breed	Sex	Owner	Breeder
1979	Eng. Am. Ch. Callaghan of Leander	Kerry Blue Terrier	D	Mrs W. Streatfield	R. Stirling
1980	Ch. Shargleam Blackcap	Flat Coated Retriever	D	Miss P. Chapman	Owner
1981	Ch. Astley's Portia of Rua	Irish Setter	B	Mrs and Miss Tuite	Mrs M. Korbel
1982	Ch. Grayco Hazlenut	Toy Poodle	B	Mrs L. A. Howard	Owner
1983	Ch. Montravia-Kaskarak Hitari	Afghan Hound	D	Mrs P. Gibbs	Mrs L. Race
1984	Ch. Saxonsprings Hackensack	Llasa Apso	D	Mrs J. Blyth	Owner
1985	Ch. Montravia Tommy-Gun	Standard Poodle	D	Miss M. Gibbs	Mrs C. Coxall
1986	Ch. Ginger Xmas Carol	Airedale Terrier	B	Mrs A. Livraghi	Owner
1987	Ch. Viscount Grant	Afghan Hound	D	Mr C. Amoo	Owner
1988	Starlight Express of Valsett	English Setter	B	Mr and Mrs J. W. Watkin	Mrs A. R. Wick
1989	Ch. Potterdale Classic of Moonhill	Bearded Collie	B	Mrs B. R. White	Mr and Mrs M. Lewis
1990	Ch. Olac Moon Pilot	West Highland White Terrier	D	Mr D. Tattersall	Owner
1991	Sh. Ch. Raycroft Socialite	Clumber Spaniel	D	Mr R. Dunne	Mrs R. Furness

Metric Conversion Table

Height		Weight	
inches	*centimetres*	*pounds*	*kilograms*
1	2·54	1	0·454
2	5·08	2	0·907
3	7·62	3	1·361
4	10·16	4	1·814
5	12·70	5	2·268
6	15·24	6	2·722
7	17·78	7	3·175
8	20·32	8	3·629
9	22·86	9	4·082
10	25·40	10	4·536
11	27·94	11	4·989
12	30·48	12	5·443
13	33·02	13	5·897
14	35·56	14	6·350
15	38·10	15	6·804
16	40·64	16	7·257
17	43·18	17	7·711
18	45·72	18	8·165
19	48·26	19	8·618
20	50·80	20	9·072
21	53·34	30	13·608
22	55·88	40	18·144
23	58·42	50	22·680
24	60·96	60	27·216
25	63·50	70	31·751
26	66·04	80	36·287
27	68·58	90	40·823
28	71·12	100	45·359
29	73·66	110	49·895
30	76·20	120	54·431
31	78·74	130	58·967
32	81·28	140	63·503
33	83·82	150	68·039
34	86·36	200	90·718

MATING and WHELPING CHART

Mated Jan	31	30	29	28	27	26	25	24	23	22	21	20	19	18	17	16	15	14	13	12	11	10	9	8	7	6	5	4	3	2	1	Mated Jan.
To whelp April	4	3	2	1	31	30	29	28	27	26	25	24	23	22	21	20	19	18	17	16	15	14	13	12	11	10	9	8	7	6	5	To whelp March
Mated Feb			29	28	27	26	25	24	23	22	21	20	19	18	17	16	15	14	13	12	11	10	9	8	7	6	5	4	3	2	1	Mated Feb.
To whelp May			3	2	1	30	29	28	27	26	25	24	23	22	21	20	19	18	17	16	15	14	13	12	11	10	9	8	7	6	5	To whelp April
Mated March	31	30	29	28	27	26	25	24	23	22	21	20	19	18	17	16	15	14	13	12	11	10	9	8	7	6	5	4	3	2	1	Mated March
To whelp June	2	1	31	30	29	28	27	26	25	24	23	22	21	20	19	18	17	16	15	14	13	12	11	10	9	8	7	6	5	4	3	To whelp May
Mated April		30	29	28	27	26	25	24	23	22	21	20	19	18	17	16	15	14	13	12	11	10	9	8	7	6	5	4	3	2	1	Mated April
To whelp July		2	1	30	29	28	27	26	25	24	23	22	21	20	19	18	17	16	15	14	13	12	11	10	9	8	7	6	5	4	3	To whelp June
Mated May	31	30	29	28	27	26	25	24	23	22	21	20	19	18	17	16	15	14	13	12	11	10	9	8	7	6	5	4	3	2	1	Mated May
To whelp Aug	2	1	31	30	29	28	27	26	25	24	23	22	21	20	19	18	17	16	15	14	13	12	11	10	9	8	7	6	5	4	3	To whelp July
Mated June		30	29	28	27	26	25	24	23	22	21	20	19	18	17	16	15	14	13	12	11	10	9	8	7	6	5	4	3	2	1	Mated June
To whelp Sept		1	31	30	29	28	27	26	25	24	23	22	21	20	19	18	17	16	15	14	13	12	11	10	9	8	7	6	5	4	3	To whelp Aug
Mated July	31	30	29	28	27	26	25	24	23	22	21	20	19	18	17	16	15	14	13	12	11	10	9	8	7	6	5	4	3	2	1	Mated July
To whelp Oct	2	1	30	29	28	27	26	25	24	23	22	21	20	19	18	17	16	15	14	13	12	11	10	9	8	7	6	5	4	3	2	To whelp Sept
Mated Aug	31	30	29	28	27	26	25	24	23	22	21	20	19	18	17	16	15	14	13	12	11	10	9	8	7	6	5	4	3	2	1	Mated Aug
To whelp Nov	2	1	31	30	29	28	27	26	25	24	23	22	21	20	19	18	17	16	15	14	13	12	11	10	9	8	7	6	5	4	3	To whelp Oct
Mated Sept		30	29	28	27	26	25	24	23	22	21	20	19	18	17	16	15	14	13	12	11	10	9	8	7	6	5	4	3	2	1	Mated Sept
To whelp Dec		2	1	30	29	28	27	26	25	24	23	22	21	20	19	18	17	16	15	14	13	12	11	10	9	8	7	6	5	4	3	To whelp Nov
Mated Oct	31	30	29	28	27	26	25	24	23	22	21	20	19	18	17	16	15	14	13	12	11	10	9	8	7	6	5	4	3	2	1	Mated Oct
To whelp Jan	2	1	31	30	29	28	27	26	25	24	23	22	21	20	19	18	17	16	15	14	13	12	11	10	9	8	7	6	5	4	3	To whelp Dec
Mated Nov		30	29	28	27	26	25	24	23	22	21	20	19	18	17	16	15	14	13	12	11	10	9	8	7	6	5	4	3	2	1	Mated Nov
To whelp Feb		1	31	30	29	28	27	26	25	24	23	22	21	20	19	18	17	16	15	14	13	12	11	10	9	8	7	6	5	4	3	To whelp Jan.
Mated Dec	31	30	29	28	27	26	25	24	23	22	21	20	19	18	17	16	15	14	13	12	11	10	9	8	7	6	5	4	3	2	1	Mated Dec.
To whelp March	4	3	2	1	28	27	26	25	24	23	22	21	20	19	18	17	16	15	14	13	12	11	10	9	8	7	6	5	4	3	2	To whelp Feb

Glossary of Technical Terms

Action   Movement.

A.K.C.   American Kennel Club.

Apple Head   Rounded or domed skull—a virtue in some breeds such as Chihuahuas, but a fault in others.

Beard   The very profuse and bushy whiskers of the Griffon Bruxellois, quite distinct from Terrier whiskers.

Belton   The lemon- or blue-flecked colour of certain English Setters, notably the Laverack strain.

B.I.S.   Abbreviation often used for 'Best in Show'.

Bitch   A female dog.

Blaze   An attractive narrow or bulbous-shaped white marking running up the face between the eyes.

B.O.B.   Abbreviation for Best of Breed.

Bone   A well-boned dog is one possessing limbs giving an appearance and feel of strength and spring without coarseness.

Breeching   Tan markings at the back of the thighs of a black and tan dog such as the Gordon Setter.

Brindle   A mixture of light and dark hairs, usually darker streaks on a grey, tawny or brown background.

Brush   Term applied to a bushy tail similar to that of the fox.

Cat-feet   Short, compact and round feet common to Terriers, and opposed to splay-feet.

Challenge Certificate (C.C.)   Award given, at judge's discretion, to best of sex of breed at some major English shows.

Champion   In England a dog that has won three Challenge Certificates under three different judges at shows of championship status. In the U.S.A. the title is awarded on points won at major shows.

Chops   Pendulous upper lips or flews common to the Bulldog, some hounds and most deep-mouthed dogs.

Cobby   Well ribbed and sprung, rather short in back, adequately muscled and compact.

Couplings   The length of the body between last rib and pelvis.

Cropped   In some breeds the ears are cropped or cut to erect shapes. It is unacceptable in Britain and some American States.

Croup   The region adjacent to the sacrum and immediately anterior to the set-on or root of the tail.

Cryptorchid   An adult dog whose testicles have not descended into scrotum. This condition bars a dog from exhibition.

Culotte   The feathery hair on the backs of the legs, as seen on the Pomeranian.

Cushion   That appearance of swelling or padding given by the full upper lips of the Mastiff and Bulldog.

Dew-claw   A claw often found on the inside of the leg and usually removed early in life but retained by some mountain breeds.

Dish-faced   A term used to describe a concavity in the nasal bone making the nose-tip higher than the stop.

Docked   Many breeds have their tails docked or cut short to specially designed lengths when quite young.

Down-faced   When the nose-tip is well below the level of the stop, due to a downward inclination of the nasal bone.

Drop-eared   When the ears are pendant and hanging close and flat to the side of the cheeks.

Entropion A condition where the eyelid turns inward and the lashes irritate the eyeball.

Fall Long hair overhanging the face.

Featherings Those long and fine fringes of hair seen on the backs of legs in Setters, Spaniels and some Sheepdogs.

Flag The fringe or feather found under the tails of Setters and some Retrievers, long at the base and shorter at the tip.

Flecked When the coat is lightly ticked with other colours, as in the English Setter, and neither roaned nor spotted.

Flews Deep, hanging upper lips.

Fly-eared Usually a blemish, in that ears which should be erect fall or tilt at the tips.

Frill That long feathering of soft hair found on Setters and Collies around the neck and longer at the throat and base.

Fringes A loosely applied term usually meaning the featherings of long-coated breeds. (*See* Featherings.)

Gay A tail is said to be gay when it is curled up over the back or erect as in some hounds.

Gazehound Greyhound or hound that hunts by sight.

Hare-feet Such feet as have the digits well separated, usually being long, like a hare's.

Haw The inner part of the lower eyelid which shows red and hangs open in such breeds as the St Bernard and Bloodhound.

Hip Dysphasia Abnormal development of the bones of the hip joint. Found in several breeds. Usually hereditary.

Hocks Those joints in the hind limbs below the true knees, or stifle-joints.

Hound-marked Fox Terriers are described as hound-marked when their body patches conform to the pattern of hound markings.

Leather The flap of the ear. The term has particular reference to ears which are pendant and large.

Mask The muzzle or fore-face, generally so-called with reference to colour: for example, a light Cairn may have a dark mask.

Merle A blue-grey mixture streaked or ticked with black, and usually seen in some Collies and Shetland Sheepdogs.

Over Nose Wrinkle A fold of loose skin dropping forward from the skull on to the bridge of the nose. Seen in Pugs, Pekingese and some other short-nosed breeds.

Over-shot When the upper teeth project beyond the lower. A blemish in most breeds, though the lesser of jaw malformations.

Parti-colour A term used for dogs of two colours *in equal proportion*, usually red and white and black and white.

Patella Luxation The knee cap or stifle slips or dislocates. An abnormality said to be hereditary and found in several small breeds.

Peak The pronounced and pointed top of the occiput which is, in the Bloodhound and allied breeds, a favourable point.

Pencillings The dark and elegant lines on the surface of the toes in some breeds, notably the English Toy Terrier.

Pied When two colours occur in irregular patches, one more than the other, a dog is said to be pied.

Plumes Whereas the brush is not always soft, plumes refer to the soft hair on the tail of the Pekingese and Pomeranian.

Prick-eared When the ears are erect, as in Chow Chows, Schipperkes, Alsatians and Welsh Corgis.

Progressive Retinal Atrophy (P.R.A.) Sometimes incorrectly called 'night blindness'. This is a hereditary defect of the eyes found in several breeds causing early loss of sight.

Puppy A dog under a year old.

Roached A dog's back is roached when it arches convexly, as in the Dandie Dinmont, Italian Greyhound and Whippet.

Roan A mixture of coloured hair with white hair as in many Cocker Spaniels—blue-roan, liver-roan, orange-roan, etc.

Rose-eared When the ear, neither pricked nor dropped, folds or twists over, showing the inside, as in the Bulldog.

Ruff The stand-off frill or apron of long (usually coarse) hair around the neck, as in the Chow Chow.

Saddle The black rectangular marking on the back extending to the upper flanks, as in the Airedale and Welsh Terriers.

Self-marked A dog is so-called when it is a whole colour, with white or pale markings on the chest, feet and tail-tip.

Slipping Stifle *See* patella luxation.

Splay-feet Feet of which the toes are spread out, as in some sporting breeds used in water-fowling.

Stern A term frequently employed for the tail, with particular reference to Foxhounds, Harriers and Beagles.

Stifle That joint in the hind leg of a dog most approximating to the knee in man, particularly relating to the inner side.

Stop The depression between and in front of the eyes roughly corresponding to the bridge of the nose.

Tongue To 'give tongue' is for a Hound to voice when on the scent. To 'sing', being a moderate tongue, and 'babble', an excess.

Top-knot The longer, finer hair on the top of the head rather like a powder-puff, as in Dandie Dinmonts.

Tricolour A term used when dogs have three colours more or less proportionate, usually black, tan and white, as in hounds.

Trousers The hair on the hind-quarters. The term is often used in reference to Afghan Hounds and Poodles.

Tucked-up When the loins are lifted up yet the chest is deep, giving a racy appearance, as in Borzoi, Greyhounds and Whippets.

Undercoat That soft furry wool beneath the outer hair of some breeds, giving protection against cold and wet.

Under-shot When the lower jaw and teeth project beyond the upper, as in the Bulldog and allied races.

Wall eyes Eyes parti-coloured white and blue, seen in merle-coloured Collies and Sheepdogs, often keenly valued.

Whiskers The beard of Fox Terriers and allied Terriers, generally elongated and tidy, rather than bushy and too profuse.

Wrinkle The loose folds of skin puckered up on the brows and sides of the face in Bloodhounds, St Bernards and Basenjis, Pugs, etc.

Index